THE INITIAL INTERVIEW IN PSYCHOTHERAPY

Psychotherapy Series

Family Therapy
G.H. Zuk, Ph.D.

Brief Therapies
H.H. Barten, M.D.

Children and Their Parents in Brief Therapy
H.H. Barten, M.D. and S. Barten, Ph.D.

Psychotherapy and the Role of the Environment
H.M. Voth, M.D. and M.H. Orth, M.S.W.

Psychodrama: Theory and Therapy
I.A. Greenberg, Ph.D.

The Art of Empathy
K. Bullmer, Ed.D.

Basic Psychological Therapies: Comparative Effectiveness
A.J. Fix, Ph.D. and E.A. Haffke, M.D.

Emotional Flooding (Vol. 1 in New Directions in Psychotherapy Series)
P.T. Olsen, Ph.D.

The Initial Interview in Psychotherapy (Translated by H. Freud Bernays)
H. Argelander, M.D.

The Self-In-Process, Vol. 1: The Narcissistic Condition
M. Nelson

THE INITIAL INTERVIEW IN PSYCHOTHERAPY

Hermann Argelander, M.D.

Translated by Hela freud Bernays

HUMAN SCIENCES PRESS
SUBSIDIARY OF BEHAVIORAL PUBLICATIONS INC.
72 FIFTH AVENUE, NEW YORK, N.Y. 10011

Library of Congress Catalog Number 75-17113

ISBN: 0-87705-248-4

Printed in the United States of America
6789   987654321

Library of Congress Cataloging in Publication Data

Argelander,Hermann
     The Initial Interview in Psychotherapy

The fact also remains that in spite of the youthfulness of psychotherapy as a technique and as a science, a vast amount of technical experience has accumulated which has to be transmitted to the student, and naturally must keep him dependent upon his teachers for a long time. The knowledge and the skills that he acquires are not merely intellectual but are based on his capacity to use himself in a total sense, and necessitate an involvement which requires commitments and convictions of a completely different type than is true in most other scientific fields.

R. Ekstein and R. S. Wallerstein:
The Teaching and Learning of Psychotherapy

CONTENTS

Foreword by Rudolf Ekstein, Ph.D.   9

Preface   21

Introduction   25

1. The Unusual Conversation Situation   29

2. The Partners to the Conversation, Their
   Motivations and Their Tasks   37

3. Setting up the Conversation Situation   53

4. The Patient, His Illness, and Its
   Meaning   63

5. Psycho-Logic, an Unusual Form of
   Thinking   75

6. The Dynamics of the Conversation
   Situation   85

7. The Material Gestalt of the Conversation
   Situation   93

8. The Aftereffects of the Conversation
   Situation   103

9. The Interview as a Threshold Situation   113

10. The Diagnostic Interview   123
11. The Therapeutic Interview   131
12. Training Problems   137

Index   147

FOREWORD

PSYCHOTHERAPY IN AMERICA AND IN EUROPE: THE TWAIN SHALL MEET

My first meeting with Hermann Argelander, face to face, took place during the summer of 1973 in the lobby of a small hotel in Frankfurt am Main. However, I had corresponded with him since my discovery of the German version of the very book I am now introducing. We exchanged reprints, and I became acquainted with the professional history of the author.

He was graduated as a doctor of medicine in 1945, having studied in Berlin; and he later worked as a chief physician at the Auguste-Viktoria Hospital in Berlin-Schöneberg. He finished his psychoanalytic training at the Berlin Institute of the German Psychoanalytic Association in 1957. Since 1945 he has been a professor, as well as a scientific member, of the Sigmund Freud Institute in Frankfurt am Main. The latter institute is a modern teaching and research institution under the directorship of Alexander Mitscherlich.

Among Argelander's publications is *Der Flieger*, a study of the psychoanalytic treatment of a flier who suffered from a serious character neurosis and for whom flying became a special characteristic of his personality. Another book, *Gruppenprozesse Wege zur Anwendung der Psychoanalyse in Behandlung, Lehre und Forschung,* deals with the application of psychoanalysis to group processes. A variety of papers published mainly in *Psyche,* the German journal for psychoanalysis and its applications, are concerned with the nature of the analytic interview, the dynamics of the first interview, work with professional groups such as members of the ministry, comparison of group psychotherapy with individual psychotherapy, and other clinical topics.

But back to the meeting with Professor Argelander. He had come to the hotel shortly after our arrival; and I might add with tongue in cheek that the meeting in that hotel lobby turned into an *ungewöhnliche Gesprächssituation*—an unusual encounter. He and I were to prepare my lecture assignments at the Sigmund Freud Institute, and I remember telling him about my first visit to Frankfurt, many years ago in 1930, during the then customary high school graduation trip. That was the Frankfurt of prewar days, full of memories of classical Germany history, beautiful old medieval buildings—the days when *Der Römer* stood still. But even then we saw the beginning of the rise of the Third Reich, and the Frankfurt of today, partly rebuilt after wartime destruction, resembles some American midwestern city.

Just as our conversation started to move from the formal introduction to the more personal encounter, we were interrupted by a young man who asked me whether I was Dr. Ekstein. He was an American psychiatrist responsible for a psychiatric clinic at the American military base. He had been one of my students at UCLA and UC Irvine and had heard lectures on psychotherapy there. He was very surprised to suddenly find me in that small hotel. Introductions were made, and I could not resist his invitation for the following morning—to lecture to the young people who dealt with the children of American families working on the military base. (After the lecture I would go over to the Sigmund Freud Institute and shift from the English language to the German mother tongue.) This American knew hardly anything about the Sigmund Freud Institute, that excellent resource for training and research, so that a bridge was being built during this chance meeting between the German and the American institutions. For Professor Argelander this encounter must have seemed almost like one of his staged scenic configurations, a kind of acting out which by chance presented the whole problem and its solution. Looking beyond my narcissistic pleasure of having the German professor notice that I was recognized far from home by an American student and, of course, having the American notice that I had been recognized—if I may play with words—by the German institute, we find that this scenic configuration hides what is really important.

The war and the distance had for many years kept me separated from and out of touch with the *Sprachkreis*, the German professional and scientific literature. Much later, shortly after the Second World War, when I started to catch up, I remember my first impression was that Germany psychoanalysis and psychiatry had not moved beyond their prewar positions. Was there really such a gap between the Old World and the New? Or was the gap just in my mind, a reflection of my having broken almost all contact with the European world? Or, was the distance much smaller? I think I found the answer. For two hours, in the American army base clinic, I taught people very much like our students thousands of miles away in Los Angeles. Then, five or ten minutes by taxi, and I was speaking to the German group. It soon became clear to me that there really was no great gap at all. Much seemed to be the same, even though the two clinical centers had scarcely any direct knowledge of each other.

I realize I was aware of all that, although only on an intellectual level, from reading Argelander's small volume back home. I had been delighted that the volume united features of both traditions and indicated that an active bridge exists for many between contributions here and there in spite of insufficient translation in both languages. For this reason I am very pleased to introduce this book to the English-speaking reader. It will prove that much of what has been done in England and the United States has already found its way to the German profession, and I hope to contribute in making this interchange of ideas more and more into a two-way street.

I am sure the translator's skill will make it possible to convey to the American reader that Argelander writes in a language free of professional jargon, even though it is clearly based on both psychoanalytic thinking and the classical Freudian tradition, and with an excellent literary quality, particularly in his beautiful vignettes in which he shows, in a few short statements which are powerful both in their descriptive and in their explanatory intent, his ability to make patients come alive.

Much of what the author offers is familiar ground to me since I, too, have been occupied for many years with teaching analytically oriented psychotherapy to residents in psychiatry and allied professions. The American literature, as a matter of fact, is part of the intellectual and clinical background to which Argelander refers. Much of our American tradition, the stressing of the pragmatic, the *how*, has deeply influenced the work of Argelander and his co-workers. The Sigmund Freud Institute, in its clinical orientation, depending on state support and health insurance coverage, is very much like American psychiatric settings. The application interview, the first telephone contact with the clinic, the preapplication interview, the intake interview, the assessment procedures, the psychiatric case study methods, the record keeping, the short-contact interviewing, the emergency interview, the one-way vision room, the use for training, the supervisory hour, all this in use in America today has become part of the work of the Sigmund Freud Institute. Perhaps this could be attributed partly to individual rediscovery, or partly to new discovery, or partly to new experiences gained elsewhere. But, in addition, there runs through the book much of the European tradition which aims at a deeper understanding, a tying-up with other clinical philosophies, and the influence of neo-Freudian and other ideas. It all has a quality of synthesis which goes far beyond the pragmatic, and which will make this small book a pleasure for the reader who wishes to read it slowly and gain from it, line by line and paragraph by paragraph.

It must also be said that the more bilingual one is, the more one realizes that each language has its unique forms of expression which often extend beyond the limits of other languages. That certainly is true for the German notion of *Sprachraum,* a notion not well translated through the English "language space." However, I not only refer to the different language spaces covered by the German or the English but I also refer to the difference in language space created through different ideological underpinnings of psychiatric and psychological theory. One of the merits of Argelander's book is that it is written in such a way that we really never become slaves of such ideological underpinnings; he permits the poetry of metaphor and of simile to take the place of those concepts which carry only pseudo-conciseness.

It is not so long ago that residents in psychiatry were taught to carry out a diagnosis by means of a patient-answered questionnaire which, together with the usual classic diagnostic methods, would presumably permit the young physician to establish a diagnosis, a name, for the emotional or mental illness. I am sure that, universally, there are still many who rely on this way of categorizing, a kind of misunderstood Kraepelin psychiatry where nomenclature seems to be the only important thing.

Argelander's first interview could be considered a *Probehandlung,* a trial action, by which the mind of the patient is tried in many ways. The doctor tries to establish a tentative picture of the illness, a tentative diagnosis possibly allowing for subsequent serious therapeutic action, or which helps us to decide that perhaps ordinary psychotherapeutic action is impossible. But this trial action is also a kind of trying out. Each of these first interviews must be considered as a way of trying out psychotherapy, a miniature psychotherapeutic hour in order to see whether a process is possible or whether the patient wants psychotherapy, and whether the psychotherapist is able and capable of offering this particular patient psychotherapeutic help. The first interview could be considered as a kind of general rehearsal which permits one to decide whether one is ready for the play, or whether the play cannot yet take place. Thus, the first hour has many a meaning, and its data allow interpretations on many levels; or better still, they require of the psychotherapist a developed capacity for such multilevel interpretation.

In this first hour we play with a variety of questions; therefore, it must contain sufficient *Spielraum* for both patient and therapist. This German word, not really translatable into English, refers to play space. The dictionary usually refers to it as "elbowroom" or "latitude." But these translations do not permit us to penetrate the deeper meaning of the German expression. Perhaps the phrase, *mit Gedanken spielen,* to play with thoughts, comes nearest to its deeper meaning. "Play" is not used here as something merely for children, playful in terms of *verspielt;* "unwilling to work and also be serious" is not what the German language has in mind here. Play, even the play of the child, should be understood as serious business, as preparation for thinking out loud or as acting out a sort of rehearsal for what later may become a serious act or decision. *Spielraum,* play space, does not allow just for elbowroom—true perhaps for a football player—but rather creates the opportunity for, as well as the rules of, the game by which something might be worked out, or prepared, or rehearsed, something for which a solution might be found. Freud spoke about "the thought" as trial action; meaning that he who thinks tries out in thought potential actions, he searches for solutions, he searches for options, for alternatives. Erik Erikson has taught us much about that play space and the play configuration.

We see that one of the complications of translating a book lies in the fact that each language has a slightly different *Spielraum,* just as it has a different *Sprachraum.*

I recall from my American lectures the use of the somewhat lifeless concept of "structure." We spoke about the structure of psychotherapy, the structuring of the first interviewing hour, the implied rules concerning time and space and fees, concerning the furnishing of the interviewing room for adults or for children; and we suggested that the structural elements determined to a large degree the process that will develop during the therapeutic interview. We could think of flexible structures, of rigid structures, or of structureless situations, but none of these expressions seem to be as rich as the German *Spielraum,* which implies both space and limit but also has richer implications. The German expression, that play space concept, permits a capacity for playfulness in the mind, not simply referring to those instinct-driven people who are perhaps prevented from acting out their desires by prohibitive inner forces. We speak now about ego psychology, the cognitive forces of the mind which can play with options, can play with pictures of the past as well as adaptive notions for the future and which, therefore, put into motion much more than the struggle between impulse and defense.

What is true for the concept of *Spielraum* also holds true for that of *Sprachraum.* Many patients have very little *Sprachraum,* very little capacity for the use of language to express their thoughts or perhaps to disguise their thoughts. One philosopher once playfully said that man had invented language in order to disguise his thoughts, but he omitted to say that man also invented language in order to think his thoughts and to communicate them. But, there are many who are unable to use words; much of what they impart is expressed psychosomatically, or is told through acting out in that very first interview described so usefully by Argelander through the concept of "scenic configuration." The participant observer, the therapist, during the first interview becomes a part of that scenic configuration; and much of his leverage as a therapist, as well as a diagnostician, depends on his capacity to grasp and to use the scenic configuration. We are involved here not only with ego psychology, but also with Gestalt psychology, a way of understanding interpretation about which Siegfried Bernfeld wrote many years ago when he saw each interpretation as the discovery of a gestalt, a configuration with a consistent but very slowly changing pattern, comparable perhaps to what we call character or personality.

Argelander gives a convincing picture of the therapist's everlasting internal struggle with the wish to know more, to diagnose better—and the therapeutic intent to help more effectively, to initiate treatment, to treat, and the like.

Psychiatric tradition holds that there should be a complete psychiatric work-up before a treatment procedure is initiated, before prognosis and treatment plan can be formulated. Argelander follows a newer philosophy, one with which I am identified, namely the necessity for a balance between the why and the how. He pleads for an equilibrium between the process of science, he pleads for verification, for the need to collect data, for the need to acquire anamnestic material, and for the forces of empathy and the truly therapeutic attitude. This combination of the scientific and the humanistic, the objective and the emphatic, the scientific and the artistic, characterize his contribution and the stage of present-day psychiatry.

I spoke about the fact that some of the linguistic problems of translation reveal that certain German expressions go further than their poorer English equivalent. But I should also like to stress that at times the reverse is the case. For example, Argelander speaks about the *Notfallinterview,* while the English language suggests the notion "emergency interview." The word *Notfall* refers, the dictionary tells us, to an exigency, while the English word "emergency" refers to an *unerwarteter Vorfall.* As I help train psychiatrists to deal with emergency situations which are so much a part of psychiatric practice in public clinics, I suggest to them that the emergency refers to phases of therapy where the patient tries to make the situation into one in which it is almost impossible to develop a process but where we are supposed to look at the patient's presentation as one point—here and there—in time. There must be, the patient feels, an immediate answer. We are faced with an emergency. I thought about the word "emergency" in terms of the original verb that speaks about something emerging. What emerges in a case of emergency, that *Notfall,* seems to be so sudden, so unexpected, that there is nothing to do but immediately react to it: fire alarms demand the immediacy of the water which will extinguish the fire. The task of the psychotherapist, however, in an emergency situation is that he deals with it in such a way that he helps the patient to see that point in time, that emergency, as part of the process, something emerging. And what is it that suddenly emerges? Usually it is a preconscious conflict creating anxiety and panic reactions. It seems to require a reaction rather than a response. The English word, then, permits us to speak about the emergency as a process, as something emerging. Thus, we turn a *Notfallinterview,* the emergency interview, into the process, which is exactly what Argelander means when he describes some of these emergency situations.

Argelander speaks about the first interview in psychotherapy as a *Gespräch,* again a word which is not well translated by the English "conversation," "talk," "discourse," or even "encounter." The word "interview" will not do either. A *Gespräch* relates to an exchange of ideas, a process, and usually it is one that follows certain give-and-take rules, written and unwritten, conscious and unconscious. In earlier days we referred to the psychoanalytic hour, which is now reserved for the standard, classical, analytic procedure. This procedure clearly indicates what the rules are for the patient and what they are for the analyst. The *Gesprächsweise* of the patient is to be free association, and for the analyst the characteristic of the *Gesprächsweise* is interpretation. Neither is absolutely consistent in using these rules, but the analytic dialogue is characterized through these two different types of communication. But this does not hold true for the first interview, even in classical psychoanalysis. However, the rules of the game and the rules of the dialogue are slowly developing. They are actually a part of the diagnostic procedure, the trial action, that *Versuchstherapie* which has to be conducted in order to reach some kind of conclusion, either to the act of ending the helping process, prolonging the preliminary exchanges, or arriving at a mutual agreement on the problem, the task ahead, and the mutual commitment to be made.

Like each book, this volume is also meant for students of psychotherapy. Perhaps for some students this actually might be—at least as far as the literature is concerned—like the first interview about psychotherapy, about the study of psychotherapy, and about their training obligations. It would not be a very comfortable book for the beginner, since it is very demanding. There are so many levels to which one must be attuned—and the task of the beginner, I believe, must look enormous to anyone used to many of the treatment remedies offered today on the psychotherapeutic market. They must seem extremely simple, actually simplistic, but they are nevertheless full of promises to be believed by him who wants to make it easy for himself. Perhaps the student must face the same problem as the patient in the first interview: the degree to which he would be willing, and the degree to which he would be able, to do something about his illness. The student now would have to come to grips with what his professional identity is to be; what kind of knowledge and skill he really wants to acquire. This book is offered to the best in our field and demands the best of each of them. It will not attract all, but those who are attracted by it will be enabled—and the learning process is an enabling process—to enter a new world, the path which Freud has opened for us, a path which has been enriched and broadened by teachers like Argelander.

RUDOLF EKSTEIN, PH.D.

Director of Childhood Psychosis
Project, Reiss-Davis Child Study
Center

PREFACE

I willingly agreed to the suggestion of the *Wissenschaftlichte Buchgesellschaft* (Scientific Book Company) that I undertake a presentation of the initial interview in psychotherapy in the light of today's knowledge after a rather lengthy work of mine on this subject was published in *Psyche* (volume 21, 1967). The present book, contrary to my original intention of delivering a purely factual documentation of what is known, has taken on a very personal note. Behind it are concealed unmistakable clues to a continuous discussion with the very lively groups of the Sigmund Freud Institute. As one can gather from comparison of the two works, current interest does not as yet permit a completely clear view of this subject. However, the recent introduction of the method by which an interview can be observed behind a so-called one-way mirror has opened up so many new problems that the thoughts in this work of necessity have to remain unfinished and incomplete. For precisely that reason, I am indebted in the highest degree to all the colleagues at our institution who participated in this common task. My thanks are due also to the director of the Sigmund Freud Institute, Dr. A. Mitscherlich, for his continual furthering of our efforts; and to the patients, from whom, in thinking over once again what took place in our conversations, I was able to learn a great deal.

Within the aforementioned framework, I have made every effort to transpose the scientific technical language of

psychoanalysis into comprehensive conversation situations
and in so doing to get along with a minimum of more or
less currently understood concepts without simplifying the
real facts of the case or becoming superficial. In this way I
hope to be able to explain to the interested reader what an
initial interview can accomplish today and what precon-
ceived opinions and false expectations are no longer appropriate. Perhaps, also, understanding will grow for the
psychotherapist's difficult and demanding activity when he
participates in such a conversation—and also the consciousness one has of one's own participation in such a
conversation. To the psychotherapist-in-training I should
like to offer an introduction to the interviewing technique
—if he has the patience, under guidance, to work through
the many-faceted levels of understanding on the basis of his
own early experiences. The demands of the training are,
rightfully, continually being raised higher and higher, so
that it is never too soon for the beginner to get a comprehensive impression of what awaits him in his future practice.

The insight into the various perception and thought
processes of the psychotherapy conversation is particularly
instructive in the self-contained first contact—the initial
interview—because one is able to get a complete overview.
Growing into technical practice goes hand in hand with
one's general training in psychotherapy. The premature
appropriation of undigested theoretical knowledge puts a
brake on the complete unfolding of the natural psychological potential for perception and perverts it. In our group
work with psychotherapists who have not yet completed
their training, we were surprised at their spontaneous capacity for empathy. This came to light during the recital of
their conversations with patients, recitals which were still of
a refreshingly unspoiled naïveté and proved in this state to
be extraordinarily capable of development. Impressed by
this experience, I have taken pains to place these simple

subjective perceptions in their proper light without obscuring complicated connections by doing so.

Despite the vast amount of knowledge that has been acquired, we in our specialty are still only at the starting point which Sigmund Freud, in his genial intuition, pointed out. Even today psychotherapy means feeling one's way into the unexplored mental or psychic regions of the human being, and preserving one's sense of awe in the face of secret and wonderfully intertwined paths in human experience without holding on to any romantic emotionalism or befuddlement.

There are certain necessary practical and didactic reasons for marking off the limits of the initial interview as a separate psychotherapeutic procedure. Nonetheless, it remains an integral part of psychotherapy. It can therefore demand to be allowed to share in all new knowledge and not to be set aside and forgotten in some out-of-the-way place, such as a mere search for biographical data. Carrying out the initial interview is and should be reserved for the well-trained psychotherapist.

INTRODUCTION

To accomplish my task of providing a more detailed presentation of the initial interview, my notion is to present not a systematic discussion of technical details or of practical directives, but rather a deepening of the concept of what an interview is. If I am successful in this endeavor, effects on the practice of psychotherapy will necessarily develop from it. In this sense I shall now attempt to draw up a modern concept of the initial interview.

The definite end product of an initial interview is a result of the working through of the informational material obtained in it. This statement as the point of departure of my reflections makes necessary a number of basic definitions. According to my observations these various pieces of information—somewhat arbitrarily separated from one another—arise from three different sources. According to where they come from, they are evaluated differently in current interview practice, played off one against the other, and, in part, even discarded as not being usable.

To begin with, we have the customary *objective informa-tion*. Here we are dealing with personal statements, bio-graphical data, and certain types of behavior or idiosyncracies of personality which can be checked at any time. These data receive their importance as psychological testimony through a constellation of data and in this way take on the character of objective information.

Thus, for example, a patient appears for a conversa-tion because there is the threat of a divorce. He has a three-year old child. His parents were divorced when he was one year old. When asked how long he has had the intention of getting a divorce, the patient replies, "For two years." All these facts can be separately checked and were provided haphazardly in the course of the conversation. From them there results a constellation of psychological testimony in the form of the following objective informa-tion: The patient, in an identification with his parents, is preoccupied with the intention of getting a divorce at the very time when his own child has reached the same age (one year) as he himself was when his parents were divorced. The motivation connected with such an identification is easily felt by a psychologist: "My child shouldn't be better off at that age than I was." From written biographical data one can glean such information without participating in a personal conversation.

The determining factor for perceiving these connec-tions on the basis of objective data is the specialized knowl-edge of the practitioner. This source of information is the one most frequently used. Its data can be checked and are absolutely reliable. On the other hand, this information contains a high degree of ambiguity. The reliability of the psychological testimony depends, finally, on the special knowledge of the field and on one's capacity for drawing convincingly logical combinations. As a criterion for the relative truth content of the interpretations, logical evi-dence is provided. The picture of a patient's personality that one gets in this way has the character of a reconstruction, and therefore is like a cliché unless it also contains the unique characteristics of an individual personality. For scientific purposes these reconstructions turn out to be extremely fruitful, but for a prediction as to an individual treatment process they have but little value. That is because perceptions are based overwhelmingly on intellectual insights.

As the second source of data, I name *subjective information*. These data can be more or less reliable. The determining factor is exclusively the significance that the patient assigns to them. The information that results from the significance connection of the data cannot be laid bare by the psychotherapist alone; it is only his work in association with that of the patient that makes it understandable. The instrument for the perception of subjective information rests solely on the professional capacity to deal with the patient in the interview situation. The information that has been gained is absolutely unambiguous, but it is very difficult to check. The criterion for its reliability is the evidence obtained from the situation, the feeling of a significant coincidence between the information and what is taking place in the situation. The picture that one gets of the patient is very vivid, but it is limited solely to the actual level of the relationship in the interview. It is very suitable for prophesying the outcome of the treatment process, but because of its individual characteristics and its being bound to the actual situation, it is very difficult to compare with other personalities. Its value as knowledge arises rather from an insight based on practical experience (see the example in chapter 1).

Scenic or situational information is distinguished from the subjective type only by a change of accent which, to be sure, is to be regarded as so significant that it can well bespeak a heading of its own. In subjective information, the data which are reported, to which the patient lends a subjective significance, still stand in the foreground. The subjective significance stands in a secondary relationship to what takes place in the situation and from it acquires its value as evidence. In scenic information, experiencing the situation is dominant, with all its feeling impulses and its imaginative end-results—even when the patient remains silent. Connecting these with the data is the secondary activity. The criterion for the reliability of the information is likewise the situational evidence, which, in consideration of the location of the center of gravity, could also be designated as "scenic evidence," for a little variety in language. Such information is practically never capable of being checked by repetition, and it is therefore discarded or not mentioned by most interviewers even though it is the richest in what it discloses regarding the prognosis of the therapeutic process. The instrument of perception is solely the personality of the interviewer, involved with and attuned to the patient's unconscious relationship field. In the second example in chapter 1, the scenic information is just about to come into being.

The reliability of the picture gained of the personality and its psychic disturbances grows with the integration of the information from all three sources, a goal that the differential evaluation of the three sources of information and the continuous conflict as to their usefulness can do away with.

THE UNUSUAL CONVERSATION
SITUATION

The psychotherapist considers the initial interview to be a first and, in general, a one-time conversation situation with a patient, limited-as-to-time, which serves a specific purpose. The concept of the goal involved in the interview is the theme of this book. The definition of the initial interview sets up definite limits for the conversation and is designed to prevent our succumbing to the alluring temptation of losing our way in conversation situations that would have to be categorized differently.

The limitations thus staked out determine the external conditions of the conversation situation and act—once they have been systematically set up—as the technical principle that structures the build-up of the conversation. The patient's looks, type of behavior, verbal communications, and what occurs in the initial interview are condensed by these external limitations into a complete testimony concerning the patient's personality. Even before the start of the initial interview, influences are at work that have their origin in

conceptions and prejudices concerning mental disturbances and their treatment, and that constitute what might
be called "prefield" phenomena. They are expressed, for
example, in the way a person makes his appearance, and
they play their part in shaping the conversation. The conversation itself, as a means of providing information, communication, and understanding, is but one component,
albeit the most important one, in this situation.

By presenting a short passage from a conversation
from a psychotherapeutic session I would like at the outset
to make clear in what an unusual way the informational
material and what takes place in the conversation situation
are intimately mixed up together.

> *Psychotherapist:*   It is exactly the way it was when you were
> 12 years old.
> *Patient:*   Of course. Now, all of a sudden, it becomes clear
> to me that it is exactly the same.

This statement had a strange effect on the psychotherapist
because just a short time before, the patient had himself
informed him of this similarity. The psychotherapist had
assumed that he was merely indicating something that had
long been known to the patient. Now he was forced to
realize that the patient was treating this remark as though
it were an entirely new idea.

In line with one's ordinary experience in conversation,
one would draw the conclusion that this patient is either
forgetful or confused. One would point out his mistake to
him or might even enter into a discussion with him as to
which party had made the mistake. The psychotherapist
does not stop at such seemingly objective observations. He
always continues to look further, to look everywhere for the
subjective significance of what is going on. Pursuing this
clue, he leads the conversation in an unexpected and unusual direction.

Psychotherapist: You've forgotten this connection, which you already knew about, and I have restored it to you.
Patient: Yes, now it occurs to me that I recently told you about it.
Psychotherapist: Well, then, if I restore it to you, you can recognize it once again as your own.

The conversation takes a surprising turn which, to be sure, comes about perfectly logically and is immediately understood by each partner in the conversation, but which must seem strange to an outsider. We are not accustomed to examine what a person says for its subjective meaning, and that is why it does not occur to us that an apparently meaningless communication can receive an unexpected significance if it is applied to the situation itself. The conversation situation includes an unusual form of perception and of thinking, a peculiarity which we do not want to lose sight of any longer.

The first part of the quoted passage from the conversation refers to the contents of the conversation, the second to the way the situation itself is shaping up. This transformation leads to the patient's being surprised at the significant content of his own remark. From this we must conclude that the patient was not conscious of the underlying meaning of what he said. The psychotherapist has only helped him to an understanding of a communication which the patient had introduced unconsciously and which he had used for the purpose of a particular statement about himself. It reads as follows: "I am unable to recognize a thing as my own. Only if someone restores it to me can I identify it anew as my own." The patient thereby portrays in the situation itself his identification disturbance, including his great dependence on a foreign object. Both partners are talking about an event that is taking place between them. The amount of knowledge contained in this unconscious information concerning the patient's disturbance is to be rated very high, and would have been lost if the conversation had proceeded differently; that is, in the usual way.

Important unconscious communications apparently have a tendency to come to light in the conversation situation. The quoted passage from the conversation used as an example appeared, as already stated, not in an interview but in a therapeutic session. Accordingly I hasten to find a completely neutral example from the literature, to emphasize what has just been stated: (1)

> A man in his early 60s, a lawyer holding a high government post, came for advice and help in a family situation. Despite the prevailing summer heat, he was attired most correctly, one might almost say formally. He began by describing the reason for his coming, and had taken great pains to prepare his "brief." In addition, he made use of some sort of legal paper to inform himself precisely as to details that were totally unimportant so far as any psychological implications were concerned, and from time to time to correct some earlier statement. He was somewhat taken aback that the interviewer paid so little attention to the papers he had brought with him. It was not until 25 minutes had elapsed that the seeker after advice got around to the subject of his family situation. When it came to his wife and the younger children and partly also to those who were already grown, he provided scarcely more than routine personal data. At this point he grew silent and gazed expectantly at the interviewer.

In this report Schraml does not give us the conversation itself but rather the conversation situation, and he describes his impression of the personality and the individual behavior of the two participants during the conversation. These were his thoughts as they proceeded:

> He was somewhat annoyed by the long and completely unproductive and tedious lecture; he had diagnosed the patient as the stereotype of the dry-as-dust lawyer, and because of it asked, in a consciously friendly and mild manner,

> whether it wasn't hard for children, especially sons, to have
> such an able and successful father, whom one could scarcely
> hope to equal, let alone by any chance surpass.

This question is an interpretation because it is designed to transmit an insight into how hard it is for sons to have such a father. The interviewer seizes upon the contents of the conversation and formulates it in the shape of a question; but the certainty that things are really thus and so, and not some other way, arises from the experience of the conversation situation itself. In it there is manifested unconsciously the significant information provided by the patient: I am such a perfect and unattainable person. That is why everybody has a hard time with me and why I have a hard time with them. That part of the question directly experienced by the interviewer, namely "Do people have a hard time with you?" does not fail to have an effect.

> The patient was at first taken aback by this unexpected and
> apparently inappropriate remark. But then his face lit up and
> he began to relate.

What is unusual in the course of the conversation comes about through the inclusion of the immediate situation and the information unconsciously provided in it. The situation itself assumes a value of its own as an informational tool because it lends the course of the conversation a significance of its own, or, as in the present case, a certainty as to its significance.

For teaching purposes, up to this point I have omitted mentioning the meaning of the contents of the conversation, in the sense of objective information or solid facts, in order to place the situational aspect in the foreground. From the last example one can deduce that we are seeking, out of the totality of the objective, subjective, and situational information, an integrated personality-gestalt, in order to put an end to the troublesome conflict as to the falsification of facts in the realm of psychotherapy. The facts obtained from these three sources of information appear to contain material that is ordinarily assessed independently, that is, in isolation from each other. The interpretation is based primarily on such subjective and situational information, the contents of which are confirmed by objective facts. In contrast to this, the integration of all the data, without any preference for individual assertions, leads to a new information-gestalt. For the psychotherapist this procedure is of existential significance because he has to bring together as equals the conscious and the unconscious components of the personality, which are recognizable in our sample; and because in the interview supplementary dynamic development-gestalts develop which are decisive in making a judgment.

In Schraml's example, the interviewer has taken into consideration the dynamics of the conversation situation with the remark that, particularly for sons, it must be hard to have such an able and successful father, one whom one could scarcely hope to equal. The dynamic development-gestalt as material for the understanding of the patient's specific personality is much more widely differentiated. It is reflected in the interviewer's long-suffering listening for more than 25 minutes and his consciously friendly and mild reaction to the patient's idiosyncrasy despite his own increasing annoyance. With some other patient, the interviewer would react differently to the same annoyance. This reaction formation—reacting in a consciously friendly fashion to an annoyance—may possibly represent a characteristic of the patient's compulsive personality.

The dynamic of the conversation takes a turn because the patient is able to make use of the interpretation and to change his behavior. From this fact there arises a further important piece of information concerning the flexibility of the structure of a personality.

Efforts at obtaining information are not to be separated from the knowledge that results from attempts at influencing and from the reactions that follow in patient and interviewer. The interviewer has to have a clear concept and carefully honed techniques in order to reflect the interplay of the submerged tensions in the reactions of both partners to the conversation and to integrate them with the rest of the data.

Today no psychotherapeutic initial interview can be considered complete without the use of these many-faceted aspects. We are involved here with a conclusion that is rich in consequences because there emanates from such an interview process a total effect on the patient which we will have a good deal to say about further on.

Chapter 2

THE PARTNERS TO THE CONVERSATION, THEIR MOTIVATIONS AND THEIR TASKS

The persons who participate in the conversation are clearly established in their roles. On the one side is the psycho-therapeutic specialist, who proves himself qualified on the basis of his education and training; on the other, the patient. The search movement always proceeds, directly or indirectly, from the patient, insofar as it concerns a previously scheduled conversation. At this point I do not want to enter into the matter of other techniques with the help of which, for example, in general medical practice, in schools or elsewhere, the unusual conversation situation is spontaneously introduced when a "patient" makes it urgent by his "unconscious" proposals. I am thinking, for, example, of a mother who time and again importunes the doctor with her child's quite ordinary illnesses so as, without directly talking about herself, to make him aware of her and her own disturbances (2).

Just as clear as the designation of roles is the inducement that gets the patient's search movement under way.

It could perhaps read something like this: "At any indications of mental illness, I consult a psychotherapist." This simple rule is contrary to the daily personal experience of how grotesquely differently medicine, psychology, and psychotherapy think about mental illnesses, what the various disciplines, schools, and universities have to say about them, and what treatment they suggest. Heretofore patients often came to us along many bypaths. Reports in newspapers, over the radio, on television, recommendations by friends or neighbors, sometimes even referrals from their attending physicians directed them to us. Of late, we also see patients, in the main members of the younger generation who, with a certain matter-of-factness, turn for help to the psychotherapist—that is, to the appropriate institution—when they notice disturbances or symptoms of mental illness in themselves that trouble them or seriously limit their capacity to perform or to enjoy. Let us hope that we are here not dealing with forerunners of some fashionable development according to which one believes oneself to be progressive by going to a psychotherapist.

But it is also possible that matter-of-course treatment has already gained acceptance in cases of mental illness; for enlightenment in this sector can no longer be held back and has already so far done away with the denial of mental illnesses that a physician would make himself universally unworthy of belief if he were to examine an impotent patient for an unduly long period of time so that, at any price, he could find an organic cause. A great deal more could be said about this psychosocial side of the motivation, but it would lie outside the scope of this book. I should like to direct the interested reader to the works of A. Mitscherlich and the literature listed there (3).

Summarizing, it must be established that today's psychotherapy patient still has to declare himself in favor of treatment and his conviction of its effectiveness in opposition to his social surroundings—or else he must hide it from them, although to a varying degree in each social stratum. This corresponds, on the part of the therapist, to the complete inadequacy of his professional set-up and the uncertainty of the conditions for his social existence. His personal prestige stands and falls with the accomplishments of which he is able to convince others. He has to win over the patient to his method as early as the initial interview, since the public is well informed about the conflict among the various schools of psychotherapy. The universities lack any scientifically recognized representation of the specialized field that engages in fundamental research on fundamentals and that represents a somewhat related attitude toward teaching. The appalling ignorance of what are the supposedly appropriate places (for example, for certification) adds to the public's confusion.

Doubtless we find ourselves in the midst of a tremendous process of social upheaval which, by the breakdown of taboos, only slowly prepares for the research possibilities that today's patient already demands, for he is waiting patiently for long lists of psychotherapeutic institutions and practices, and in intimate psychotherapeutic conversations shows himself to be well in advance of the concepts of his time and of public awareness.

Imbedded in this sociopolitical background and in no way uninfluenced by it, the interviewer must assert what his task is. Fortunately, the motivation of the individual patient is better than social cliché would depict it, because suffering is connected with it. In their short study, M. Muck and J. Paál (4) have declared that it requires the combination of the stress of suffering and motivation to provide the best conditions for psychotherapeutic treatment. The early assumption that "whoever recognizes symptoms of mental illness or who suffers from it ought to consult a psychotherapist," thereby proves to be inadequate—quite independently of what public opinion is with regard to psychotherapy. This assumption is modeled on the notion that mental disturbance, too, can attack human beings the way an infection does or a digestive or hormonal disturbance, and should, correspondingly, be handed over to the psychotherapist as the appropriate place for treatment. The patient, the one burdened with this disturbance is, to be sure, the directly implicated victim; but in any other respect, he does not have much in common with the disturbance. Even when there is the definite stress of suffering, this clear and understandable motivation will not create favorable prognosis for treatment, even if it is legitimized by public opinion.

This statement is difficult to explain without entering into a long disquisition on the essence of mental illness and the body-mind unity of man. At this point we ought to remind ourselves that we do not want to lose sight of the unusualness of the psychotherapeutic conversation situation. The patient in Schraml's example had family difficulties and, logically, consulted a psychotherapist. He apparently prepared himself very thoroughly for this conversation; one can say he had a good, conscious motivation. In the conversation situation, it became clear that his behavior, which was derived from this motivation, represented precisely the problem that had brought him into difficulties with his fellows. Accordingly, the conscious motivation has to be measured on an evaluation scale which is oriented to an understanding of the psychologic dimension and to an insight into psychic connections.

M. Muck and J. Paál evaluate such statements as "The patient wants an analysis in order to learn to understand his problems better" or "The patient does not want to be treated with medication but by psychological means" as the expression of a strong, conscious motivation (+), while such remarks as "The patient is seeking help," "The patient expects a solution of his problems from us" and "A clearing-up of the external situation" are the statements of a person with lesser motivation (0), and such remarks as

"The patient would like to have physical treatment—he believes that he doesn't have any problems" are those of a man with too little motivation (-). These examples are taken from actual practice and can be multiplied as desired. Their evaluation has a practical meaning, yet it does not precisely solve our complicated problem of motivation; because the unconscious motivation is missing.

In Schraml's example (page 8), the patient reacted to the interviewer's intervention—"People have a hard time with you, because you are so competent and successful and one can scarcely hope to equal you"—with a change in his behavior; he became more human, and his description of the persons close to him became more alive. One has got to make clear to oneself that this change did not necessarily have to occur. The fact of the change testifies to the fact that the patient was not a rigid character in a legalistic stereotype, but unconsciously offered as his problem this stereotype with its background psychological significance such as "perfectionism," "unattainability," "superiority"— and when he was approached about it, was able, relieved, to let the subject drop. This patient, accordingly, was unconsciously much better motivated than his falsely understood conscious motivation would lead one to expect.

While the conscious motivation could be read from his remarks during the conversation, the unconscious motivation was disclosed by the arrangements in the unusual conversation situation itself. By "unconscious motivation" in this context, only unconscious elements of will and of decision that are connected with the disturbance are referred to, which indirectly let us recognize a readiness for treatment; not the unconscious wishes which are attached to the treatment. Suppose we assume that this patient possessed a compulsive-perfectionist character, that he had in his family already come to know the negative aspects of this character and had distanced himself somewhat from them. For this reason he was now leaving his legal papers at home, was presenting himself as markedly spontaneous, and in what he said and in his expectations was giving the impression of being well motivated, but that he was not able to produce anything new as the result of an intervention and would remain rigid and monotonous in his corrected behavior. In other words, he could not really change himself to conform to a situation nor provide any unconscious communication. Despite the psychological insights that he had gained, which even correct his general behavior, the unconscious motivation remains unsatisfactory.

Thus, in psychotherapy, motivation includes both the conscious and the unconscious portion, because it is only both together that produce a clear picture of the justification for any claim to psychotherapeutic treatment. That is why motivation includes the personality structure and a series of essential personal capacities in varying degree. They must be present—or at least must be capable of being awakened in the conversation situation—whenever psychotherapy is sought as a form of treatment in which the two partners to the conversation want to help each other gain insights in an unusual situation in order to draw conclusions from them.

Good motivation is indirectly supplemented by intelligence, awareness of reality, capacity for psychological thinking, ability to be active, insight into one's illness, capacity for empathy, inner flexibility, the ability to form an object-relationship in an actual situation, and so on. The more we delve into these connections the more clear it becomes that external conditions such as social consciousness, enlightenment, and a scientific attitude cannot be seen as separate from the nature of the individual personality. Unconscious motivation and the illness stand in a reciprocal relationship to each other. Beyond that the illness can be typified even on the basis of unconscious motivation, when one is permitted to deal with the concept of illness in such a broadly conceived fashion.

On the basis of a considerable number of protocols of interviews, I have tried to work out this intertwining of conscious and unconscious motivations on the one hand and illness on the other as a form of typification (5). This typification helps us to a rough, practical orientation which has proved valuable but which requires a more widely differentiated working up. As I now turn to this attempt at typification and try to draw up its first results, I must once again emphasize that we are concerned only with formulations of the material from the prefield of the interview. That is, illness is defined here solely on the basis of the material of this prefield.

1

The first type of patient I call the "sent-on-ahead" or the "pushed-ahead" patient; for he comes not on his own initiative but under pressure from another person—a parent, a spouse, or so on. Apparently other people are more interested in his treatment than is the patient himself. Frequently his appearance is preceded by several telephone conversations with these others. No sooner is the interview over than the others would like to know what the patient's examination has revealed and what, in detail, is now to be done. These patients' conscious motivation is naturally weak. Also, according to definition, this type lacks any personal stress of suffering and any readiness for treatment or readiness for conversation in general. His "sickness" consists of his being presented as the symptom of a social sickness; and here "social sickness" simply means that the visible phenomenon of being sent on ahead arises from the dynamics of a sickness that includes several persons and thus proceeds in a social field. This definition does not touch upon the basic problem of the social involvement of mental illness in general; this sickness can be compared with an infection that involves a number of people and holds them in its power. But not all those who are infected feel themselves equally sick; rather they agree among themselves as to who, in their opinion, is sick and should be sent to the physician. Sometimes the patient is the victim of this sickness, and the others feel relieved at his expense. That is why, in this particular constellation, every attempt at treatment has got to fail; if it succeeded, the entire treatment structure of the other parties, which has been stabilized in this way, would be destroyed. But sometimes the patient who has been sent on ahead also embodies an alarming signal of the presence of a disturbing sickness-dynamic affecting these several persons, so that the readiness for treatment of a single individual or even of several persons is basically greater than one assumes.

At the beginning, I looked upon this type as prognostically unfavorable, but a later rechecking made me suspicious. From a total of 100 unselected interviews, I was able to isolate 5 cases of this type and was amazed that 4 of them, after the wind-up of the entire investigation procedure, were considered suitable for psychotherapeutic treatment. Accordingly the unconscious motivation must have worked itself out more favorably than the external conditions had led us to assume.

This type requires an interview technique of its own. The technique is primarily a matter of freeing the patient from his passive role and of directing him toward himself and his own active participation in the social sickness. It develops that behind this type very varied personality structures are to be found that have been overplayed by the dynamics of the social milieu and thereby have been over-formed in external cliché fashion.

When the relatives prove too disturbing to our occupation with the patient because of their interference, it is recommended that they, too, be offered an appointment in order to discuss with them what the sickness means to them personally. By following this technique, which at all costs makes a point of avoiding any discussion concerning the patient, one is able to make the most interesting observations. On purely semantic grounds, we designate the first person to be examined as the patient and the one seen later as the relative. Often, then, the important question arises as to which of all of them would be the suitable "patient" for treatment—a posing of the question with which we are sufficiently familiar from child therapy. Especially for interviewers who have difficulties in working in the conversation situation and therefore tend to put too much value on objective data, and in a sort of taking sides with the patient, paint a picture of the "terrible relatives," a corrective conversation and a personal impression of the relative are very instructive. Often it is enough to have a colleague conduct this interview with a relative and then to have the colleague and original interviewer discuss the results of their interviews.

Naturally it is an easy matter to approach this sickness in the social field with more direct methods, for example, to observe the married couple jointly in the conversation situation and to turn one's diagnostic perception onto what takes place in the conflict between the two; that is, onto their marriage. The subject of the investigation is then no longer a sick person, but a sick marriage. This type of patient, by definition, broadens the psychotherapeutic work-field, which in many institutions is being studied with great interest (in marriage therapy or family therapy, for example).

2

Another type of patient, one who enters into the conversation situation in an unmistakable way and exerts a strong influence on it, I have called the "demanding" patient.

Often he already has a number of attempts at treatment behind him and keeps the interviewer or his institution busy in advance with telephone calls or correspondence in which he makes his demands and wishes known. Thus, for example, he would like to have an elderly, especially experienced, and gentle interviewer. Such high demand is in contrast to a lack of personal involvement. At the time set for the first appointment, he often does not show up or arrives too late; then, at the end of the conversation, it is only with difficulty that he can tear himself away from the interviewer; he would like to call on him for all sorts of helpful services.

This type of patient is so engrossed in his own self that he can scarcely imagine himself in the interviewer's place. That is also why he is quickly offended or disappointed, feels that he is being misunderstood, and sometimes complains. When it is time for him to pay, in extreme cases he is nowhere to be found, or else he doesn't have any money at his disposal. For the most part it is only at this point that the actual poverty of his real existence, which is hidden behind his excessive demands, is divulged. The discrepancy between his demanding behavior and his personal possibilities is the criterion for this type of patient. Behind this behavior are concealed persons with disturbed relations to reality, who, despite their great demands, actually lead a miserable existence. In the conversation situation they are unreliable and uncontrollable, and for the most part arouse reactions of pity, which spoil a correct evaluation of them. Sometimes the interviewer, on the basis of induced feelings of guilt, sees himself inclined to introduce therapeutic measures which frequently end in disappointment. Not seldom, this type exhibits psychopathic traits. In this case, they commit large or small acts of tactlessness and provoke a hidden or an open rejection. The patient has an unfavorable effect on the interviewer. For the most part the interviewer is tempted to guard against this feeling because the patient, on the basis of his fate, rather deserves pity or a readiness to help.

These patients come up with dramatic psychological syndromes and have a colorful and lively history of illness, but despite their suffering, they do not have any real insight into their illness at their command. They seldom agree to what a well-planned treatment calls for and are also, when looked at critically, for the most part not suited to psychotherapeutic treatment in the psychoanalytical sense. Although behind this type there are concealed various personality structures with very diverse syndromes, the principal manifestation is a psychopathological disturbance in narcissistic development with exaggerated behavior as regards demands and an objective self-evalutaion that is false.

With the relatively high number of 15 patients that I was able to locate in the 100 unselected interviews, the distorted feeling with respect to tact was a principal indication. Apparently this sign is especially easily discernible as a characteristic by the interviewer. Ten of the patients had already had unsuccessful treatments behind them. These patients are not able to turn any negative experiences to their own benefit but continue to project, tend to act-out, and remain unreliable. Often they have very self-willed notions with respect to their illness and its treatment; but, on the other hand, they are too easily won over for a treatment. They are, however, unable to develop any constancy and cannot make constructive use of any disappointments or frustrations. Their apparent psychological understanding is very strongly tinged with emotion.

3

A type of patient opposite to this dramatic and demanding patient is the "undemanding" or "unproductive" patient.

His symptomatology consists exclusively of functional syndromes. With respect to his resistances, behavior stereotypes, ego or rather life limitations, he has no awareness of the problem. That is why he affects us as colorless, inflexible, and in his unconscious psychological conversation manifestations, uninteresting and tiresome. This type cannot charm and captivate the interviewer in the conversation but instead spreads a paralyzing or unpleasurable atmosphere about himself and is repressed in what he does say.

Although we already knew this type and were aware of his or her peculiarities, yet in the monotony displayed by this patient we were almost brought to despair when, in a psychosomatic study of amenorrhea, we came upon a "pure culture"(6). The determining criterion for this type is the isolation of the symptomatology into a functional syndrome, for example, constipation, stuttering, anorexia, and so on. In these patients the entire emotionality appears to be frozen into this particular symptom. The conscious motivation is, for the most part, based on the negative experience or previous attempts at somatic treatment without any conscious insight into the illness as regards its psychological connections. These patients are the great deniers of their own psychic life; they are emotionally numb and without any real demands for the realization of their personal needs.

In the interview situation they erect a barrier around themselves and are completely incapable of any activities of their own directed toward the goals of the conversation. As in all typification, we also find among them transitional forms that come to light in the course of the conversation or following it, and only then give us a chance to recognize a rich and abundant inner life. The technique of the interview must be directed at this resistance, yet it remains a laborious undertaking if one is not interested in this specific form of resistance. In the latter case, one comes upon unconscious motivations which give this resistance behavior a meaning of its own and yet can allow the patient to appear suitable for treatment. In a supplementary rechecking of 10 unproductive patients after the close of our investigation procedure, I had to declare that 7 of them were considered suitable, although these patients did not give us a chance to recognize any conscious insight on their part into their illness nor any readiness for treatment. This group of patients requires, as early as the initial interview, psychotherapeutic work to combat resistance; in other words, it incorporates the type in which, in the course of an interview, it is the most difficult to separate the diagnostic and the therapeutic activities from each other—a problem we will take up more fully later.

4

A last group to be separated out, and one that apparently is in the process of growing larger, consists of "enlightened" patients. Their motivation is determined by what they know, the degree of their enlightenment, and their need for more knowledge. For the most part this type of patient has already been working on himself and uses an appropriate vocabulary which comes from the literature, his occupation, or his earlier treatments. In contrast to the demanding patient, he does not flirt with this knowledge of his; he takes it seriously, because it is based on strong intellectual needs, it strives for completion, sometimes even for absolute perfection. This highly trained and mostly very differentiated intellectuality is in contrast to the locked-in, stunted emotional life that is very difficult to get at. With this patient's gifts and his well-trained intellect, his outlook is fully justified and corresponds to his personal readiness to become involved. Once convinced, he is ready to go along with everything that is required. He is willing to have his treatment cost him something and makes every honest effort to make use of his own possibilities in its behalf. To many, this type appears as the ideal patient—until it turns out that behind his intellectual motility, his real interest, and his convincing conscious motivations, almost insurmountable barriers screen off his emotional life. The barriers are insurmountable because the object relationships that are borne by the emotions are prematurely suppressed and are still bound up with the infantile anxieties that accompany them. So it very often happens that separation anxieties permit the possibilties for satisfaction in the object relationship to retreat for the benefit of admiration for the gleaming intelligence and the documentation of its power.

This type is often found in high and responsible positions. The patients do indeed learn from the conversation, but they use their knowledge for the strengthening of their narcissistic position. Often they have exceptionally emotional partners who are irritated by the deficiency in their emotional life, reproach them for their lack of spontaneity, yet, on the other hand, marvel at their self-control and their superiority. In general, these patients do not underestimate the psychotherapist when they are convinced of the quality of what he does. For the most part, they themselves feel the insufficiency of their emotional life and are therefore grateful for every sincere help they are given.

These four groups of patients, insofar as they appear capable of being separated to some degree on the basis of external interview findings, in my judgment represent some 30 to 50 per cent of the patients who come for an initial interview. The remaining patients turn out to be a mixed form, or else they represent types with which we are not yet familiar.

The peculiarity of the psychotherapeutic interview situation accordingly has a challenging effect on personality indications. Its external constellation, with its demands, its goals, its concepts, and the conscious and unconscious motivations of the patients calls forth phenomena which, in the manner of announcing oneself, of transmitting information, in one's attitude toward the illness and in the uniqueness of the way the conversation is carried on, are condensed into typical configurations. These, quite independently of the individual personality, permit certain predictions that have a high value diagnostically and prognostically.

The psychotherapist is very careful to note phenomena that precede the actual conversation or accompany it. However he must not permit himself to be bound by them to definitive individual diagnoses. His observations, in addition to the attempts at defining the type, often serve to give the correct meaning to the often ambiguous contents of the conversation. Here the word "correct" has to do with the degree of a higher validity in the arrangement of the material for the purpose of understanding the personality and its disturbances. Later, we shall see how this integrative activity of the therapist is carried on in the most varied levels of the situation, and how the many facets of its material are thereby furthered.

Chapter 3

SETTING UP THE CONVERSATION SITUATION

How this unusual conversation situation is brought about is a matter of technique. The conception of the technical procedure is properly directed towards the goals that the interviewer has set before him. For this part of the initial interview they are as follows: We try to set up conditions so that the patient not only can communicate or express himself, but beyond that, can reveal the personality disturbances, which we have to know in order to be able to pass judgment.

In the course of a normal medical examination, the history is taken first. After that, the physician sets up an examination plan to obtain objective findings. In this way somatic medicine arrives at a diagnosis. In the psychotherapeutic initial interview, we take the history and simultaneously find out how things stand objectively. While we direct our attention to the contents of the report of the illness and, in the light of the history, deliberate on diagnostic possibilities, we observe the personal form that the presentation takes. It unfolds in the course of the conversation and provides an opportunity for laying bare the personality disturbances, for becoming oriented as to their extent, and for getting a feeling as to how they can be therapeutically approached. Let us think, for example, of Schraml's patient (page 8) who disclosed his personality disturbance in the course of the conversation. From the report we can gather how the interpreter was impressed by this disturbance. He observed it and finally tested out how it could be approached.

Introduction into the conversation situation is effected in three steps. The first one we could designate as the technique of the prefield. The therapist attempts, by means of what he has learned, to deal with the general concepts and expectations and in this way to gain an influence on how the particular patient reacts to the conversation situation. The influences of the prefield on the course of the interview are very considerable; for they have their origin in cultural and social opinion formations, prejudices, and changes in style, and are therefore only to a limited degree to be reached by efforts at explanation. We see that in the case of Schraml's patient this prefield influence makes itself felt in a type of behavior that is specific to the personality and without regard to the situation and to the person of the interviewer, and holds sway for a considerable period of time.

The nearer the patient gets to the interview situation itself, the more effective his personal concepts and expectations get to be. In this way our influence grows. This can be summed up in a simple rule: We respect the complexity of the prefield, leave all activity to the patient, do not press him to do anything, and give in to his claims, wishes, and demands as far as our sense of reality permits. We recognize it as the patient's right to urgently request an appointment for an interview, not to appear at this appointment, and then, after perhaps half a year, to put in an appearance. We know that there are reasons for this behavior that lie in the patient's personality, in the conditions of his life, in his indecisive character, in the ease with which he can be influenced, or in his specific anxieties. In this way we learn to know the patient by taking cognizance of and evaluating his behavior as an important piece of preinformation and putting it to use when the patient renews the contact. This, for essential reasons, absolutely necessary attitude toward the patient allows for a good deal of elbowroom, but it has its limitations in the particular interviewer's reality; that is, on the particular elbowroom which the interviewer can arrange for the patient on concrete grounds.

I made our limit clear at the Sigmund Freud Institute after a few years, refusing to grant appointments for interviews which led to ever longer and longer waiting periods. Appointments that were not kept led to what might be called a dry run, that is, a reasonable waiting period beyond which one could no longer be responsible to a still-waiting patient. As we are a small group with limited possibilities for appointments, we did not at this point alter our technical attitude, but we did introduce a preinterview conversation procedure so that in a short orientation conversation we could select and discard all those patients who from false expectations—that is, by having come to "the wrong address"—wished to take advantage of our help and thereby of our time. In this way the prefield is organized as either an advantage or a disadvantage under pressure of the interviewer's current reality. In doing this it is important to reach a compromise while retaining this technical principle.

We grant the same freedom to the patient in the choice of his interviewer. Some patients come to us with very definite positive or negative notions as to what kind of person the interviewer should be. Often an interviewer is recommended to the patient by an acquaintance or a colleague, and the patient expresses the wish or even the demand that this particular interviewer should examine him. If our situation permits, we accede to such wishes and requests and use them in the framework of our total view of the patient. In an institution, the following of this technical principle can lead to grotesque configurations: A patient had an appointment with a woman colleague, walked into the office, took one look at her, and declared that he would not be able to talk to her. Later he asked for another interviewer, because this woman had appeared to him to be too young. We respected this wish, and later we came to understand why he had behaved so negatively and why he had not given our colleague any possibility at all of taking this unexplained reaction and of working with him on it for a while at least.

This short sketch of the prefield and the technical principle anchored in it permits us to recognize that what is unusual in the conversation situation comes to the fore even in the prefield, and that the interviewer behaves differently in it than one would expect in everyday life. Instead of reacting as though personally offended, he aims to understand and not to miss any opportunity to learn something important about the patient. That is why the interviewer must grant the patient leeway to keep going, to express himself as far as reality permits. Despite the request that the interviewer should set only limitations that can be realistically explained, we grant him, too, a personal freedom of decision. It would be absurd to have an interviewer who, contrary to his professional intuition, reacts in an offended or outraged fashion towards a patient and cannot get rid of this feeling. That is why he, like the patient, must have the right to be able to decide against a particular conversation situation. If, in exceptional cases, he does not take advantage of this right, his own embarrassment will grow, and the quality of the results of his examination will be lessened.

Opening up elbowroom not only is an appeal to the patient; it also protects both of those who are taking part in the conversation against going beyond their inner conditions and letting themselves in for a situation with which they can no longer cope.

The personal analysis as a definite component of psychotherapeutic training puts the interviewer in the position, in the patient's interest, of renouncing as far as is possible the exploitation of this elbowroom. The more inadequate his training has been, for external reasons, the more elbowroom the interviewer, too, must be able to demand for himself.

The importance of personal freedom of decision can plainly be seen in our training groups for physicians, theologians, pedagogues, and others who do not go through an analysis. In their training it serves as an unwritten law that each participant himself decides when and with whom he enters into the "unusual conversation situation." On the basis of the reports of what takes place in their particular practice, we show them the critical point of time at which their decision for or against an intimate conversation will have to be made. This problem can be set forth by way of two extreme examples: A physician gives a woman patient a gynecological examination. He can find no physical illness but stumbles upon remarks and behavior in his patient that lead his attention away from the physical examination in a psychological direction. Now he has to decide whether he wants to make use of these observations in an "unusual conversation"(7). The same holds true for a pastor, when a woman member of his congregation comes storming into his house at a late hour in a transparent garment, demanding help. In this respect, it is much easier for the professional psychotherapist. He himself can determine the time and the outside limits for the unusual conversation, even though in doing so he has to conform to the necessary ground rules.

The second step in the structuring of the initial interview is taken up with the planned preparation of the situational conditions. The conversation requires, beyond an agreed-upon appointment, a period of time for it to reach its unusual form. (In Schraml's example, it took over 25 minutes until this phase was reached.) The interviewer must plan for a somewhat extended time span in which he will not be disturbed by telephone calls or other tasks. In our experience, an initial interview lasts about one hour. It is not enough simply to "give the patient a quick look," as people sometimes unreasonably expect. Under certain circumstances an experienced psychotherapist can get an important impression even in a short time, but it will be impossible for him to arrive at a comprehensive formulation concerning a situation that is anchored in the here and now, and which in its uniqueness cannot be postponed. Casual contacts leave their traces behind in both participants and make the coming conversation situation difficult. In consideration of the complexity of the initial interview, no one should take such additional difficulties upon himself unless it is absolutely necessary. In the above-mentioned preinterview proceeding (page 30), we limited ourselves to purely factual information and avoided any "unusual" conversational development.

As a rule the interviewer, in his awareness of his demanding task, must set up a time plan in which he has the necessary time at his disposal without interruptions and can provide the inner readiness and concentration to be able to cope with the procedure of the conversation situation. The habits and experiences of a prolonged treatment cannot be transferred to the situation of the initial interview. The one-time conversation has got to find a meaningful ending and does not permit of later corrections. Insufficient attention, lack of time, and impatience can provoke dynamic developments that have a negative influence on the formation of a judgment.

Besides planning for the time, the place also has a certain part to play. It should not have a forbidding effect, but should exude a certain sense of quiet and ease. In it are reflected the undisturbed intimacy and lack of pressure of the conversation, in which thoughtful pauses are inserted for reflection. During these phases the room where the conversation takes place must not distract or disturb, and external noises or conversations should not be noticeable as interruptions. Here, too, reality sets its limits. In the creation of the external situation, we are no longer so fanatically anxious to create a pure experimental situation in order to act on the patient like an empty mirror in which he can observe only himself. Today we are not concerned with creating utopia by such effects. The patient's preconscious perception espies a great many personal details which we ourselves may no longer notice. This hidden communication has its own part to play in bringing about the situation and does not permit of any neutral objectivity whatsoever. On the contrary, these personal details represent points of contact onto which the "unusual situation" is structured.

The make-up of the location in which the conversation takes place cannot conceal any individual traits, but it should do justice to the basic requirements of the initial interview and should help to make the atmosphere of the conversation clear to the patient—which he can make use of to his own advantage as a preparation for trust, openness, intimacy—understanding, walking-along, thinking-along, and empathy. I do not want to enter further into details, as these questions are too closely connected with the external conditions and the individual personality of the interviewer. A local psychotherapist who practices in his own home and engages in artistic pursuits will provide a locale that is quite different from that of a member of an institute who, in this respect, has only a limited space at his disposal. There is no place in the initial interview for any manipulative arrangements.

The third step in the introduction of the conversation situation requires a certain bearing on the part of the interviewer. This is much more difficult to bring about because it takes shape only with the professional identity of the psychotherapist and with his solid training.

The form that the conversation takes grows with the interviewer's experience as to the meaning of the situation, becomes more complete with the extent of his personal knowledge, of his inner certainty and maturity, and is, finally, rooted in the interviewer's total personality. The technical principle of this fundamental attitude works in two directions. The interviewer's sole purpose, namely to understand the patient, encourages him to lay aside his everyday conversation experiences and the restraint that is connected with them, and lays him open to what is unsuaul in the situation. The initial interviewer does not criticize, he does not judge; on the contrary, he accepts everything as it is offered to him and searches only for its meaning. That holds true for banal data as well as for the most painful intimacies and exciting actual facts. Most patients, faced with this sort of attitude, open up surprisingly fast and speak with a sense of relief about things which they otherwise would entrust to no one. This attitude, evidenced in such types of behavior as quiet patience, a turning toward the patient, and unbiased attention and interest, has a decisive influence on the depth of the conversation. Shame, pain, and anxiety in the face of intimacies are no longer realistically justified when this attitude is relatively safe against being disturbed. Instead, they appear as a phenomenon of the unconscious theme of the conversation situation, and through it they gain an individual value of their own with the character of testimony concerning the patient's personality.

The other side of this encouraging attitude is the frustration that is kindled by the expectant attitude, the thoughtful silence, the controlled spontaneity, and finally by disappointment at the absence of any direct advice. For the most part, it takes a long while for the patient to be able to understand what the interviewer is in a position to give him, what value the interviewer's words have for him. Whether this frustration works out in a disturbing fashion depends finally on the preparation of the prefield, the motivations and the distance which the patience is able to win for himself, and for his own "material." Against blind demands that quickly turn into acting out and that cannot become insights, the psychotherapist is powerless. That is why it is of extraordinary importance to set up clearly the limits of the procedure, to make them visible to the patient, and to see that they are acceded to.

If an interviewer believes that he can conduct a conversation under all possible conditions and is able to understand everything, he easily falls a prey to acting out. There are circumstances under which unconsciously he can act in accordance with the patient's wishes, can become dependent on him or even enter into a pact with him in a misunderstood sense, and by doing so, support him in his endeavors and demands. Sometimes in this way he can be useful to the patient, but the actual significance of the initial interview has already been lost. Younger colleagues, especially, underestimate the value of such technical rules and, undisturbed by them set themselves up beyond them—until, after several painful experiences, they recognize their own limitations. Rules are only directives. The extent and limitations of their binding force, every interviewer has continually to determine anew for himself and try out and test for their justification. In this way a personal technique is built up that contributes a great deal to one's own security and professional identity. The attitude which has been personally adopted and which becomes ever more deeply imbedded takes on individual traits in the interviewer's behavior, in his language and gestures. To be sure, unnoticed stereotypes can be built up from them that run the danger of becoming rigid and hard to correct.

Chapter 4

THE PATIENT, HIS ILLNESS, AND ITS MEANING

After this detailed study of the requirements of the initial interview, we turn now to the patient and his illness.

The patient's illness is a pathological process within the psychic system. It stretches to include the subjective and objective, the internal and the external, the conscious and the unconscious life and experience spheres of the human being, changes these in its own capricious way, and finally causes suffering within the person involved or with his surroundings. Mental illness is the manifestation of a process which is firmly fixed in all reaches of the human personality, which leaves its mark on it from earliest childhood on, and which often determines the singularity of the personality. That is why this process is closely related to all the maturational and developmental phases of life.

In a simplified form, we can think of this process somewhat as follows: The inexorable maturational and developmental phases necessarily call for changes which cast doubts anew on an equilibrium that is already established at a specific phase. They demand a new adjustment of the already changed internal and external conditions, and to that end set in motion a process of change, the task of which is to master this adaptation. No sooner, for example, has the infant played its way into a harmonious relationship to its mother than the ripening processes disturb him in his equilibrium; for he begins to perceive the mother in a different way, whereby she assumes a new significance for him. Parallel to this, the mother changes her attitude by adapting to the more mature conditions of growth of her infant. In this way, often with painful experiences, a new stage of maturation must be adapted to, for which new forms of relationship are adequate. These demands in the course of a lifetime continue with every new environment, every newly arrived at developmental phase, every new partnership, and every new task. Such a critical threshold is noticeable even in earliest childhood in the transition from the total-care symbiosis with the mother to the demand for partial autonomy and bodily control.

Another critical difficulty can be created by natural external conditions when a sibling is born into the family. Let us describe graphically, as an example, the situation of a two-year-old child. It has already reached partial independence from direct bodily closeness to the mother and discovered new possibilities for a relationship with the father. At the birth of a sibling at this particular period, the heretofore existing equilibrium of the family is disturbed, since the newcomer now occupies the central position. This change can favor progressive or regressive developments. Progressively, the tendency towards growing independence with a closer relationship to the father can be strengthened. The regressive development consists of a harking back to methods of behavior that have already been surmounted, which compel a greater turning to the child on the part of the mother. The child wants, once again, to be fed by the mother, wets or soils itself, cries when the mother goes away, and so on. The forced changes in behavior have, as a result, specific, unconscious behavior patterns which, under certain circumstances, can become pathogenic. They can manifest themselves in latent personality deformities or in symptoms of childhood diseases.

The origin of mental or psychic illness is to be sought in the critical periods of childhood development, quite independently of the particular time of their appearance. It cannot be my task, at this point, to deal in detail with the concept of mental illness in its relation to developmental psychology. By my examples I wanted only to open the way to a basic understanding. We shall now turn to the subject of the initial interview in which a patient, together with his illness, claims our attention. We want to observe his illness without prejudice just as he presents it to us under the conditions prevailing during the initial interview, and step by step get to the bottom of them, as far as our theme will permit:

Opposite me a woman of about 40 is taking her seat. Just now, on the way to my office, I had the feeling that her step seemed wooden. She impresses one as a large person, rather thin, wearing a simple, gaily colored summer dress with a white sweater over it and some blue grapes made of carved wood as earrings. She is a typical blonde with pale, unpigmented skin on which a pair of dark horn-rimmed spectacles stand out in sharp contrast. She just does not know how to bring out her looks to the best advantage— apparently she tends rather to emphasize her external defects. In conversation she impresses one as being very lively, with a definitely pouting, stubborn undertone, which also determines the theme of the conversation. At the same time she weeps continuously without knowing the reason for doing so and uses one paper tissue after the other. In this way she does not make an impression befitting her age, but rather embodies something childishly defiant and resistant—yet, at the same time, helpless.

At the outset the impression is in opposition to another picture that she provides in the course of the conversation. Her views seem to be very sensible. One keeps understanding her better and better, and recognizes her as a competent woman who obviously is capable of accomplishments. On the basis of her reliability, according to what she reports, she is frequently called on to help others in word and deed.

In these few data we come upon two aspects of her personality which elicit our interest and call for different emotional attitudes towards the patient. The awkward, stubborn girl at most calls for our pity, while the sensible and competent woman impresses us favorably.

The patient has an external problem in the form of her illegitimate, dark-skinned child whose father, a native of Africa, returned to his homeland after years of study in Germany. For twelve years the son lived with her parents who, grown old in the meantime, can no longer adequately cope with the lively boy. During these years the patient had created an independent position for herself. Now she would like to take the child to live with her, but she cannot definitely make up her mind to do it and in all her deliberations gets into a regular panic in which she no longer knows what she should do. Because of the necessity for a change of schools for the child, she consulted a school psychologist. The latter suggested that she consult our institute. On the basis of her talk with him, she realized that her wish to take her own child to live with her would arouse personal conflicts. Although she, according to our definition, originally as the mother was the relative of a "sent-on-ahead patient," she is now—consciously—well motivated and in her panic is experiencing a tremendous amount of suffering.

Now let us try to put her disturbance in its proper perspective, after we have learned something about her.

The patient has been suffering for a short while from an increasing state of inner panic which is related to an external problem, taking on the responsibility for her own 12-year-old son. The nearer the date which she had set, on the basis of objective considerations, approaches, the greater becomes her panic and her indecisiveness as to the necessary preparations to be made and the steps to be taken. Behind this external problem with her son, there comes to light in the interview situation, as an unconscious part of her personality—a sullen, weeping child who seems to be having difficulties of her own. Basically, isn't the patient perfectly justified in her anxiety at the prospect of her own responsibility for a child who is a difficult one for many convincing reasons, if, with the childish part of her own personality, she is not able to cope adequately with the problem? She needs a psychologist for her child and a psychotherapist for herself. This fact leads to the suspicion that here there are "two children," in competition with each other. As confirmation of our assumptions we begin by questioning only the informational material put at our disposal in the interview.

Suppose we remain with our last statement. Why does the patient, unconsciously, enter into competition with her own child? From our clinical experience, we could assume that she has a younger brother. As a matter of fact, her only brother is two years younger than she is and always understood brilliantly how to get his parents and others in his surroundings on his side, while the patient, overly good and wooden, inwardly full of sullen feelings of envy, grew up in his shadow. When he was born she was two years old, that is, in the obstinate phase. At this stage of development, according to our assumptions, she remains resentful—of course, only in that part of her personality that regulates her relationship to her love objects. That is the impression she made on us when we got our first impression of her: a sullen girl who conspicuously makes herself ugly, gives the impression of helplessness by doing so, and arouses our pity.

The meaningful content that is congruent with these few striking facts brings us close to the assumption that one can leaf through an illness like this as though it were a book, if one has sorted out the right threads which render the inner logic of what occurs in the illness transparent. Accordingly we continue to bare the facts. Does her son's nature resemble that of her brother? The patient says, "My parents completely spoiled my child who, with his dark skin color, always takes life from the sunny side but cannot be brought to engage in any continuous accomplishments." Thus the son like the brother, possesses to an excessive extent qualities which the patient hasn't even a trace of. Instead, she is a competent worker and draws other people to her through what she does and through her readiness to be helpful.

On the basis of our deliberations, the patient's external conflict slowly becomes transformed into an inner one; for behind the visible facade of her behavior, there emerges a personality which is incorporated in another person and which seems to be quite meaningful for the patient. One could entertain the suspicion that the birth of her brother had a traumatic effect, because the patient left to him—and later on to her own son—the happy and unburdened relations with her parents, while she herself, without any transition, stubbornly turned away from them and from her own needs for affection. Even today she still holds everyone at a distance with this curdled stubbornness of hers. She makes every loving approach impossible and, at most, arouses pity.

This step-by-step reformulation of the external conflict with her brother and her son into an internal one makes things difficult for many interviewers, although it is of significant importance for the diagnosis and the treatment. That is why our question reads: What inner component of the patient has gone over to her child as its representative? This question we can pursue only from the point of view of the child—or rather from that of the brother—because we do not get any information from the patient as to her feelings of affection. We have got to turn back onto her these remarks of hers about the persons who have taken on these functions.

The brother knows how to turn his fellow men in his favor. When the patient makes this remark, she adds that he was able to show his feelings and could enter into emotional relationships with others. Accordingly, the brother represents feelings and needs which are directed towards others; but in the case of the patient, because of her sullen behavior, they do not come to light. She uses her stubbornness, to be exact, as an inward barrier, in order to become more independent of her emotions. In this sense her sullenness is an exaggerated transitional phase on the way to her own autonomy. However, the patient remained stuck in this phase and even today still misuses sullenness out of an inner need, because she has at her disposal no other possibilities for coping with her rebuffed emotions. Our patient's sullenness is the product of a deformed personality development, since it could not be surmounted in a manner suitable to the phase or adequate to the age but up to the present has got to be submitted to for the suppression of her emotions. Her sullenness is almost petrified, and that is why the patient gives the impression of being wooden. When the brother left their parents' home to get married, the patient had the idea that her parents would keep her tied to their home. This notion was the motive for her to rush away from there. From our knowledge of the inner conflict, we would now say: When her brother, the legitimate external representative of her emotions, removed himself from the picture, her own emotions toward her parents began to be active in the patient, so that at this late date she might take advantage of her opportunity. "Her emotions held her bound to her home." This formulation shows the true motive for her fear that "my parents want to hold me bound fast at home."

From sullenness against these rising emotions, she immediately turned away from her parents and hastily found a suitable partner from a far-distant continent, who obviously was to take over the brother's function, which was now missing. If we recall the qualities she mentioned in describing her son, we can gather correctly that he was extremely suited for this task. The patient misused her partner as the external representative of her own rebuffed emotions. His strangeness guaranteed the necessary distance from her parents and herself. From him she had her child, who at the present time has become the bearer of her emotions. When the time came for her to follow her child's father into his homeland, she found many perfectly justified reasons for not leaving with him and instead dissolved the relationship.

According to the inner logic of her barely perceptible sickness process, it could not be long before she entered into a new intimate relationship. Again she chose a foreigner, this time a European, about whom she alleges that he was very similar to her son, because, like him, he was an extraordinarily charming man. "In his case I slowly came to realize that he was an unreliable person upon whom I could not rely." She had used the same words to characterize her anxiety about her son. This expression reveals for us the actual reason for denying her own emotional world, for putting herself at a distance from it, and for experiencing it only in the case of others, whom she finally condemned. When her second partner wanted to return to his own country, she dissolved this relationship, too. Despite this, her growing child was so taken up with the relationship, that he still looks upon this man as his father. In the patient's opinion, this notion of her son's can be corrected only with great difficulty, by which she clearly brings out how much she denies his dark skin color.

In the meantime, her son had grown sufficiently in his own personality so that he was able to take over the role of her brother in relation to her parents. Protected in this way, the patient built up an independent position for herself with the help of her profession. Under these circumstances, her life went along without any real emotional involvement, that is, visibly limited; while her son, as the representative of the emotional life which she had rejected, was well taken care of by her parents. With dismay she now had to become aware that this happy solution is coming to an end and that in relation to her son the dangerous feelings are coming back upon her like a boomerang. Now we understand that the panic has its source not in the real difficulties of the external situation—this patient could easily cope with them —but in her own inner conflict, which becomes manifest through the external changes of her life situation.

To make this internal conflict clear, I will supplement the report of the interview with some passages from the psychological test which, on the basis of another method, is directed much more immediately at the patient's internal situation.*

On the whole a relatively correct judgmental picture, so that one can say that the patient's ego structure rests on a sound basis. The accent definitely lies in emotional conflicts which she tries mainly to handle or to combat in that she limits herself in the field of her perceptions to what is concrete, what is immediately present, in order not to allow fantasies to arise. Avoidance, in addition to repression, plays the decisive role. The solution through avoidance of relationships does not, however, fully succeed, as she at the same time is very needful of having something or someone to lean on. So as not to become too anxious she tries to keep her relationships down to as harmless a niveau as possible, in that her concern is with security and protection only, not for sexual

*I wish to thank my colleague, G. Worm, for turning the test findings over to me.

needs. A further and more important defense mechanism is externalization, in which the son probably plays the central role in her fantasy as the bearer of something dirty and bad. That is why she does not succeed, either, in breaking away from her parents—that is, from her childhood. In her obstinacy, to be sure, she puts forward such a loosening of ties in one of the stories in the test, but on the blank page she explains how she came here in daddy's car.

Findings: We are dealing here with a phobic-hysteric structure, in which the defense against repression is supported by avoidance of relationships, that is, avoidance of the perception of certain needs. In the defense what is of concern are essentially infantile sexual impulses, which, as the result of emotional regression, are connected with something dirty, in which the son appears partly as the bearer of this impulse that is defended against. In her object-relationship she regresses to a childish sexual level, in which an attempted stubborn turning away from the parents conceals the oedipal disappointment which probably lies at the basis of it.

This test finding, independent of the interview, coincides completely with the perception of the illness gained at the initial interview, which was worked up as has been described above. Without entering into the details of the process of the illness, we have taken pains to discover something as to the patient's illness and its deeper meaning solely on the basis of actual data from the initial interview. In doing so we have gained an insight into a technique which brings the illness as an external, conflictual experience back to its intrapsychic dimension, from which the actual pathogenic effect arises which manifests itself in the symptom of the incommensurate panic. From this we learn how narrow the effect of the solutions of external conflict can be as a therapeutic measure against the processes in mental illness. Nonetheless we must often be satisfied with them.

This example clarifies still another problem. With the assumption of the cost of psychotherapy by insurance companies, a new discussion begins as to the definition of mental illness. In our patient's case, the illness and her personal fate are difficult to separate. The acute phase of panic must be accepted as illness in the medical, the psychological, and the insurance-law sense. It is, however, not the result of any sort of effects from the outside comparable to the so-called physical illnesses. The exclusively pathogenetic agent is revealed, with the realization as to its subjective meaning which the patient gives to the apparently external conflict. Only an insight into this sense connection compels us to draw the conclusion that an intrapsychic process latent since her second year of life is functioning here, which not only created the preconditions for her present illness but has contributed to the development of a personality structure that is characterized by limitations in the unfolding of her life and her decisions as to her possibilities in the way of experiences. Where the line is to be drawn here between illness and personal fate depends on a decision with respect to measurement—that is, it depends on one's definition. It is influenced by the cultural norm, the state of one's knowledge and perception, and not least by the money, which the individual, or society, is ready and in a position to lay out for the treatment of the illness.

Chapter 5

PSYCHO-LOGIC, AN UNUSUAL FORM OF THINKING

In the previous chapter we went deeply into the subject of a patient's psychic illness on the basis of events in her life. Elucidation of the significance of the child as the bearer of the external conflict constituted the bridge to our understanding, on the background of her disagreement with her brother who was two years younger than she. The disease mechanism and the symptom of panic it produced were explained as the patient's misuse of her brother and her child as the representatives of her own feelings, which appeared to her to be unreliable and which she had therefore rejected. She got into typical conflicts with these external objects, relieved herself of her anxiety at their expense, and in this way made herself secure against her own emotional life. This defense system to a great extent limited her leeway for experiences, because her emotions were unable to come into play.

If now we look back and consider how we arrived at this knowledge, we have to state the following: We examined the material in the interview with *our* eyes and established significant connections that were not known to the patient herself. Strictly speaking, in our working over of the material we have lost sight of our patient's present condition because we have not yet given consideration to the actual situation.

That is why we now turn once again to the patient, to transmit our newly gained knowledge to her. We can prophesy with certainty that the patient will not be in a position to understand the significance of what we know and to confirm it. Such a confrontation regularly calls forth defense reactions. Presumably this patient will rationalize and offer a good many explanations for her difficulties with her child, or else withdraw, feeling herself misunderstood, and will weep even more than she has been doing. The patient thus will display behavior that is in opposition to our best intentions, and this is what we call a resistance. She will perhaps admit that her most comprehensive, most patient and most convincing explanations are just that, but she will not be able to evaluate them for herself in their true significance. This fact should occupy us a bit further, for this resistance appears senseless to us in the highest degree because it renders useless our efforts to let the patient participate in the knowledge that we have gained, and can even bring about the failure of the interview.

The interviewer has two techniques at his disposal for circumventing such disturbing resistance:

1. The interviewer avoids any disagreement with the patient. Dedicated to the goal of the initial interview—that is, of getting as much information from the patient as possible for making a judgement—he omits every intervention that might disturb the collection of data. If the patient irritates him, he as far as possible does not react to this actual behavior, but concerns himself exclusively with the material presented. By the use

of this technique, the role of being the one who does the informing falls to the patient, while the interviewer works over the contents of the information in an interpretive way. The patient is pleasantly affected by the interviewer's understanding and reticence and feels a sense of relief at this type of conversation. The two are ready to part amicably and keep each other pleasantly in mind. Most interview conversations are carried on along the lines of this model.

At the outset, we emphasized that we do not merely engage in a conversation; we take the total conversation situation into consideration. It is precisely through the conversation situation that that which is unusual in the initial interview first appears. That is the reason why our decision is not rendered in favor of this conversational model, although it is the most convenient and the most pleasant to handle. The knowledge that is acquired in this way is, to be sure, logically correct; but it need not necessarily be relevant to the illness process. It is possible that the picture we have of the illness includes only marginal manifestations of what is taking place pathologically. The patient is the only person who can correct our view of his mental or psychic illness, and that is why we feel unconvinced without his confirmation.

2. The interviewer works through the informational material in conjunction with the patient. To begin with, for every interpretation that he makes the interviewer first gets the necessary unconscious confirmation from the patient. In doing this, he confronts the patient, though not with a comprehensive explanation of his view of the meaning of the illness as it has been sketched above. Instead, the interviewer limits himself to

remarks, interpretations, or questions which reflect the meaning only of the *immediate phase* of
the conversation. Every single phase of the conversation, including the situational aspect, is examined in this way for its unconscious meaning
content. Here, too, the patient furnishes the necessary information by what he says and by his
behavior. Beyond that, the patient directs the interviewer's perception by the interviewer's direct
reactions to the patient's behavior and by the
patient's spontaneous further conversation,
which now, besides its informative function, takes
on a corrective and confirmatory character. The
patient takes on a dialectic function in the conversation, which is the precondition for an understanding of his illness.

Let us take as an example an unproductive
patient who now sits before us, believing that he
has reported everything of importance with respect to his illness, grows silent, and waits for
some activity on the part of the interviewer. At
this point, one can overplay the nonproductive-
ness of the conversation situation and can now
put questions to the patient which, according to
all our experience, he will answer easily and willingly. In this way we receive information as replies to our questions, but no more than that.
With the help of these data we can try to explain
something about what is taking place in the illness, but it will be something that we have not
really understood. Instead of this, suppose we let
this unproductiveness have its effect on us, pay
attention to all the accompanying manifestations
that appear in connection with it; then connections will suddenly dawn on us that open up a
new approach to understanding that up to this

point has been blocked. We sense the difference between obstinate, passive, or anxious silence, make a remark concerning it, and often find to our amazement that this silence is not so painful and unproductive as we had really assumed. In reply to a question that does not avoid the phenomenon but includes it, we receive unusual answers that throw much more light on the patient's illness than would the answers to a whole list of the other type of questions. The interviewer's frequently expressed complaint that he receives too little material is completely unfounded. Exactly the opposite is the case. In general the great amount of data surpasses what the interviewer can manage in the way of integration, because he cannot equalize their many-facetedness so that a clear and central picture is delineated of the patient and of his illness.

I should now like to work through the data in our example step by step and in so doing show why the interviewer has placed the clarifying significance of the brother into the foreground and has given no consideration to the personalities of the parents and the patient's relation to them—although we know that these were at least as important for bringing about the disturbance as is the brother. The interviewer was older than the patient, so that there was no reason with him not to allow the memory of the brother and the unconscious disagreement to come alive in the conversation with the interviewer's help. The various phases might be separated as follows:

1. The patient presented herself to the interviewer, as has been described on page 39, and called forth an emotional attitude on his part which, despite pity, was rather on the negative side.

2. The negative emotional attitude was strengthened by the manner in which the patient referred to her son. She showed no understanding whatever for the difficult situation of a dark-skinned child, who, in such a culture as ours, urgently needed charm in order to be able to assert himself against the primarily negative or even hostile attitudes of his fellows and to win them to his side. The interviewer's entire sympathy was directed at this poor child, so friendly and of such a sunny disposition.

3. At this point the patient began to weep without let-up, using one handkerchief after the other. With increasing feelings of pity, a part of the interviewer's positive feelings again turned to the patient sitting opposite him. This recurrent emotional movement turned to a sympathetic attitude toward the patient as the interviewer discovered, in addition, the sensible and capable woman she was. This submerged, diminished rejection of the patient, the turning toward the misunderstood child, and then the turning back to the patient before him gave rise to the preconscious thought —that is, to the thought that at this point was not yet clearly grasped consciousnessly—that here two children were rivals for the favor and attention of a parent.

4. Completely dominated by the effect of her external conflict, the patient, in reply to a question, said that she already sees it surely coming about that the boy would be spoiled and pampered by all the neighbors in the house and that she alone would be left with the unpleasant task of making him attend to his homework. This formulation and the already noted absence of a maternal attitude confirmed the thought that, in the patient's

conflict, an older sister is objecting to having to care, over and above her own duties, for a younger brother who exploits his advantages in a shameless way.

5. In reply to the further question as to how the patient really would like the relationship to her son to be, she declares that what she longs for is a comradely relationship with him, where they would mutually support each other and be able to live together in friendship and harmony.

6. Only at this point did the interviewer receive the information that the patient has a brother who is two years younger than she. He had her tell him about the brother. The resemblance between what was presented concerning the relationship to the brother and to the son now brought with it the assurance of the absolute correctness of the interviewer's understanding up to this point.

This information now, of course, takes on a different significance because in a flash it throws light on the experience with the patient in the conversation situation and releases a feeling that it is significant evidence—not evidence in the sense of a logical resemblance to the material, but situational evidence, as I called it in an earlier work of mine (8). Situational evidence is something that I abstracted from clinical evidence, which occurs when data concerning illness are so worked up with the help of clinical experience that they call forth a feeling of logical evidence (such as the procedure in the preceding chapter). In my view and experience, situational evidence possesses much greater value for psychological understanding. Independently of my clinical studies on situational evidence, my colleague, A. Lorenzer in his theoretical studies of perception came to the same conclusion. He writes:

> The surest foundation for psychoanalytical perception is the patient's participation in the situation. . . . The analyst takes part in the life-practice of the patient by means of a functional regression. He takes the language corresponding to the practice from the practice itself, and returns what has been shut out of the communication, again in connection with a community of language. . . . The participation in the patient's life-practice achieved through transference and countertransference lays the foundation for both presuppositions as to a reliable perception by way of "scenic understanding"; it makes possible the precision of meanings and the anchoring of understanding in factual reality. (9)

The "psycho-logic" that we need in order to understand our patient's illness is not exhausted in making accessible the logical connections, but takes on validity only in scenic understanding. It acquires its meaning when we are able to bring the material into harmony with the scene in which we are participating with the patient, and when the situational evidence confirms the correctness of our procedure. The patient not only reveals, by his information, an impression of the unconscious play of forces that his illness brings about; he also presents it directly as a scene in verbal communication with the interviewer. This creative capability for scenic formulation of the unconscious conflicts I bring together with a specific ego function, calling it the "scenic ego function"—a marvelous gift that human beings possess.

Psycho-logic as an unusual form of perception and of thinking thus comes into being because, through a dialectic process with the patient and beyond, connections between data in the situation itself come alive, and by way of language and behavior communication constitute a scene, the understanding of which, by way of a regressive participation, is made possible only by a working through of the data which does justice to the true dimension of the illness. With this explanation we have once again taken up the thread from our first chapter and we shall never again lose sight of it.

The essence of mental illness lies in unconscious intra-psychic processes, which can be made accessible by way of an actual scene with a conversational partner. We know that the patient, with the help of his scenic ego function, exposes these processes to view as early as in the initial interview, and we ought to wait until our understanding is capable of playing along with them preconsciously.

In an initial interview, preconscious perception and thought processes come to an end unbelievably quickly and later on scarcely allow themselves to be recaptured in their entirety. That the interviewer always knows more than he can put into a protocol is a rule at our institute. That is why, as a matter of principle, we give the interviewer the opportunity to structure this impression in a summarizing group discussion with colleagues after the interview is over, and in this way to be made ready for an understanding of the illness.

The statements formulated here are by no means new. Freud, as early as 1905 in his case study of "Dora" (10), had become convinced that the reconstruction of Dora's illness and her memories would have presented themselves quite differently if he had been able better to recognize the material that was connected to the details concerning himself and his situation. Thus the material receives a new arrangement and a new center of interest through the inclusion of the actual scene. It is new for us to have to learn to bring the neglected initial interview technically to that standpoint which today's science can expect from it. What is perhaps new also is the surprising insight that, as early as the first conversation, processes of this kind are at work, which we know elsewhere only from psychoanalytical studies of long-term treatments. Our ignorance of these processes is to be explained by the generally known fact that only very few persons have brought a real interest to the subject of the initial interview. Even Freud himself never took up thoroughly in a work of his own the subject of the first contact with a patient.

Chapter 6

THE DYNAMICS OF THE CONVERSATION SITUATION*

The preceding chapters have prepared us for the fact that in the initial interview we are dealing with a very complex and highly differentiated situation, the systematic researching of which alone will provide us with the material that we must have at our disposal for the understanding and the judging of mental illnesses. We want, at the outset, to continue somewhat further with this feeling our way into the situation, before we try to gain a general view of what considerations and techniques we still have to use in order to arrive at a proper evaluation, beyond this individual experience, of the patient's personality as a whole.

The basic framework of the initial interview, the creatively formulated scene, is basic information for the understanding of an alien happening. According to its nature, it has a dynamic or a drama of its own, which it feeds

*Originally published as *Zur Psychodynamik des Erstinterviews* [On the Dynamics of the Initial Interview], *Psyche* 20:1966, p. 40.

from unconscious sources. In a well-conducted interview with a well-adjusted and well-controlled patient, this dramatic scene passes as though "underground across the stage" and presupposes well-schooled perceptions in order to get into usable contact with it. The dramatic accent, however, often monopolizes the entire interview situation and then completely dominates the scene when patient or interviewer get to acting out, dealing with the dramatic accent in barter fashion. Often the unintended increase of the dramatic is the result of a technical error; sometimes it indicates that the patient is not suitable for conversation treatment, or that the interviewer is still not sufficiently experienced.

On such an unwanted occasion, the true dimension of the latent dynamic comes to light. It releases its real series of values when, torn from its lifelong well-practiced defense mechanisms, it becomes independent in its dealings and hopelessly submerges the situation.

In the work quoted above, we tried systematically to study the unconscious dynamics of the initial interview from the viewpoint of a second conversation situation that follows. In one instance, the unconscious dynamic turned into a scene of acting out. The woman patient came to her second appointment with the unconscious motivation of having her revenge on me for the disclosures she had provided in the first conversation, which she experienced as a vanquishment. She poured out tirades of hate against me, and intimations made up of whole cloth. Thus she declared that I had had her come for the second time only because I had been unable to evaluate the first conversation correctly. In this way she forced me, against my will, to join her in acting out. Afterwards I was annoyed at myself for having let myself be carried away in this manner. In my later conversation with my colleagues, the reaction of pity for this pathetic patient carried considerable weight, and one of them finally declared himself ready to take her on as a patient in psychotherapeutic treatment. After only a short time, he had to break off treatment because the patient attacked him personally in similar fashion, did not adhere to any rules of the game, and in her blind hatred became impossible to deal with.

Such extreme cases are relatively rare, and in their behavior and acting out these people reveal their own psychopathology. One must at some time have experienced such dramatics to be able to get the proper picture of the series of values of the interplay of forces connected with and bound to the illness. Furthermore, one must guard against any prettification of the unconscious dramatics to which my colleagues, too, were susceptible, until one of them convinced himself through his own observation.

Let us turn now to another example in order to become better acquainted with the dramatic element in its great diversity. I shall limit myself to a presentation of the key scene with its more immediate circumstances.

Before this patient appeared for her prearranged appointment, I received a friendly letter to which was appended a detailed life history in which, very factually, the most important events in her life were set forth. The patient had been an illegitimate child. Her father, a man in an important business position, died before she was born, without any knowledge of her existence. When she was still a very young infant, she was adopted by a decent laboring couple and very carefully brought up, with a conspicuous tendency to let her become something special. In her energetic way and her undisguised manner of speaking openly, the patient did, to be sure, seem to be identified with this solid milieu and to be epitome of it. But according to her statements, even as a young child she had created a world of her own in which, apart from the rest of the family, she read a great deal and engaged in fantasies as though she had had an inkling as to her unusual position in the family. Her intellectual development, contrasting markedly with that of her surroundings, is to be understood as the result of an unconscious family romance; that is, as the result of fantasies concerning her particular descent. For this, perhaps the way her adoptive parents behaved towards her provided a certain realistic cause. In her later life, her fantasy turned out to be the actual reality, after she found out that her adoptive parents, as a matter of fact, were not her real parents. Her personal capacity to cope with her unusual fate lasted until she was grown. She married a man of a higher social position and became active in a demanding intellectual profession. Her two children are now both married.

Now she was sitting opposite me. After a pause at the outset, she asked whether she might smoke. When I said yes, she laid a pack of cigarettes on the table and took one out. I quickly reached for my lighter, but she was already ahead of me, lit her cigarette herself, and declared in a matter of fact tone: "Thank you. I look after myself." In everyday life, this sort of a proceeding belongs to the trifles, the personal marginal accompaniments of a conversation, but in our unusual situation this apparently insignificant trifle can be of considerable importance as information. I had understood her "she always looks after herself," and thought of the factual life history, her energetic and independent manner, and now listened further as she, pointing to her mass of papers, began to talk. In a strange way she began by discussing a textbook in great detail and explained to me her attempts to learn something from this book about herself and her problems. This phase of the conversation went on for some time and I was deliberating that on the one hand, she was so independent and was a person who "looked after herself"; on the other, however, she appeared to me as though she were an existence on paper, something out of books. This impression grew, because in her later conversation she also remained completely reasonable and permitted no emotions of any sort to come to the fore.

Unexpectedly, I noted an irritation within myself, believed that I would no longer be able to get close to this stone wall, and formulated to myself, "I'm afraid I just can't do anything for her. It's a matter of a very diffuse feeling of helplessness and resignation." Exposed to this, it became clear to me that the patient had to present herself as being so independent, self-sufficient, self-contained so that she could cope with this helplessness of hers which I myself had just felt, a helplessness which comes to grief in the face of the paper facts of reality, in thinking of which, her birth certificate and similar papers came to my mind.

Here, in consideration of our theme and the anonymity of the patient, I shall refrain from repeating the details of her actual disturbance situation, but shall instead steer toward the climax of the scene. Although other matters which stood in an interesting connection with our central theme came to be spoken of, nothing had as yet changed in her behavior and in my inner emotional mood. As the patient was lighting her second cigarette, I felt the need to light one myself, although as a general rule I do not smoke during an interview. As I did not find a cigarette in my pocket, I began, to my surprise, to feel annoyed that the patient had not offered me one from her own full pack. Fortunately, I then remembered that I had a full pack in my briefcase. So I leaned over, broke open the pack, lit a cigarette for myself and said, on the basis of a sympathetic understanding of the current scene, "I look after myself, too." These words expressed my temporary identification with the patient's tendency to look after herself, which represents an attempt to overcome the helplessness and resignation which I had become acquainted with in my own self, just now, for a short period. With considerable certainty I assumed that the patient would accept this considered yet clearly confronting remark of mine and through it be able to realize the effect on her partner in the conversation.

To my surprise she became thoughtful and fell silent for so long that I began to have serious doubts as to whether she had not taken this remark as a tactlessness or as an ill-willed attempt at getting even with her. Then I noticed that a change came over her, and that the rest of the conversation created a completely different atmosphere in which the two of us understood each other very well. She had, then, perceived on the basis of my remark that in her strivings to be independent she had completely overlooked the needs of her partner in the conversation— a fact which played a very important role in her actual conflict.

This little episode is supposed to show that even an insignificant scene with the patient is structured not only for the purpose of learning but also possesses its own dynamics to which one can very easily succumb if one allows one's feelings to enter, if one is not able to hold them under strict control. What is determining for the communication is the appropriate yet clear formulation and the accompanying tone of voice which gives the contents their meaning, to which the patient can tune in. The massive confrontation corresponded to the patient's undisguised style of speech —to which she reacted with absolute assurance, although I myself had begun to have doubts.

A further example of quite a different sort is brought us by the character of a relationship, the dynamic of which has great diagnostic value.

A still-youthful patient in a blue suit, a green knitted jacket and a red tie—a round boyish face, ears that stick out from his head, appears friendly and forthright. Advised by a friend, he has come in order "to find himself." Behind these fine words undoubtedly there lies something infantile, naïve, although the patient indulges in thoughtful pauses and thus at first makes a very favorable impression.

By looking carefully, however, one notices that he is not really thinking, but is obviously busying himself with something else. He keeps looking to the side as though there were something there that bothers him. His remarks are clear and thought through, they show deliberations of his own. Thus he feels that he is being managed by his parents who accompany him everywhere like a shadow, and who smooth his path for him wherever he goes. He wants to be independent of them but is unable to surmount this hurdle of a shadow because he always keeps needing them, for he always turns out to be found wanting. Because of his ugly ears, he had been the butt of teasing in school as a child and was unable to stand on his own because of being a "softy." What this softness of his really means and why he is so dependent on it is something he is unable to bring out, although he continuously tries to do so and has already talked to his friend about it.

I find myself increasingly irritated by the fact that he keeps glancing sideways into the corner. In reply to my direct question of whether there is anything there that bothers him, he asks if he might be allowed to change seats with me. We change seats. Immediately his behavior changes, as though I had now passed an examination and had won a position of trust—he had earlier regarded me very skeptically. Although he appears to be trustingly inclined, there does not seem to be any personal relationship to me in the picture. Accordingly his change in manner must be caused solely by the new spatial constellation that I granted him. In the same way, he apparently experienced himself as being managed by the anonymous shadow of his parents.

In the friendly atmosphere brought about in such an impersonal way, he tells me of strange things that surprise me, less because of their content than because of the way he tells them. In great detail he talks of walking in his sleep and his nightmares. He ends up with a dream in which he experiences himself as being superdimensional in size and he and his mother play ball with the universe's moons and suns. Innocently and naïvely intimate, he does not have any feeling that his trusting proximity alienates me more than did the previous distance that I was able to cope with.

That is why this scene has such great diagnostic significance; because the inability to fill a distanced object relationship with adequate emotional content turns into a situation in which, despite a childlike trusting proximity, "worlds" separate us from each other. Behind the amiable frankness, a childlike naïvté is paired with grandiose narcissistic fantasies, the diagnostic value of which clearly arises from the way the scene is taking its course. Natural defense mechanisms become superfluous because of a spatial change and give way to a regressive movement, the dynamics of which, together with its contents, are first required to provide the correct information. The diagnosis of a borderline structure is, on the basis of the interview alone, practically to be obtained only from the dynamics of the scene.

The evaluation of the test material confirms this view and describes the experienced scene in somewhat different words:

> The Rorschach test is excellent, especially with respect to the dark plates, because of the patient's attempt to draw back onto grandiose, narcissistic self-images which, however, remain cold and unfruitful. . . . Deep separation anxieties compel the patient to seek for safety and defense. He is unable to find either. The retreat into the passive role leads to a denial of reality, which he in turn tries to compensate for by fantasies of grandeur. Thereby the object relationships always get more and more lost.*

---

*I thank my colleague, M. Muck, for supplying me with the test results.

Chapter 7

THE MATERIAL GESTALT OF THE CONVERSATION SITUATION

I have chosen the word "gestalt" because I am convinced that processes in the Gestalt psychology sense have a vital part to play in the consideration of the theme on which we are now about to embark. The framework of this book and my own inadequate knowledge in this specialized field do not permit me to go into this interesting problem in detail. That is why I should like to limit myself in a pragmatically simplified form to illustrating this phenomenon by an example.

In the meantime we have learned that in an initial interview material is provided in the form of information concerning one's fate, memories, configurations of relationships, actual conflicts, worries, complaints, dreams, and much, much more. Beyond that we have learned that these pieces of information are not given by mere chance but that they take their places in order around a scene, which, as the nucleus of the initial interview, represents a particularly important source of information for the under-

standing of the occurrence of a mental or psychic disturbance. This scene arranges its own dynamic, the play of
forces of which, in its true dramatic order as to size, become
recognizable when, in the scene, language communication
is separated from insight by both dealing and dealing coop-
eratively with it; in other words, when the scene deterio-
rates.

Beyond these important realizations, the material con-
denses its sense structures into a gestalt of its own. It
reaches out for increasing validity. A patient's continuing
spontaneous statements do not result from a fortuitous
succession of various themes; they are rather to be regarded as structural elements which join together to
become a meaningful construct, if one does not disturb the
patient's presentation process. One can ascertain the particular significance of individual pieces of information later,
when the gestalt has become visible. This fact furthers the
technical consequences that one should not proceed hastily
in linear fashion in grasping the meaning of the data and
in so doing pay attention only to the newly acquired information, but rather should proceed in a circular fashion, in
order to also bring earlier data once more into view. We
bear data in mind even when we have only an inkling of
their meaning and work with them only when they become
recognizable as structural elements of the sense connection. This technique corresponds to the well-known basic
rule for analysts: to consider all information by the patient
with the same equable attention and not to critically select
individual bits; and to wait until all of them acquire their
own meaning. In this connection, I call to mind a remark
of my patient's at the beginning of the conversation, "I look
after myself." The individual meaning of this early piece of
information was only gradually opened up, after "looking
after oneself" could become tangible as a defense mechanism against dependence, helplessness, and resignation.

The sentence we quoted permits of a number of interpretations; only a single one, however, applies to this particular patient. There are presented to the interviewer, together with the patient's mental or psychic disturbance, unconscious configurations in the form of an individual gestalt. The gestalt was formed when, in the course of the patient's life, unconscious events collided with the preconscious perception processes, left their traces behind, and in their adaptation to internal mental economic conditions and external reality, formed themselves into such an individual gestalt. In our conversation situation, these configurations prove to be phenomena of the illness, psychopathological deformities. They have drawn life limitations in their wake and can even become derailed into a sphere of complete withdrawal, as in the example that follows.

From a protocol made some time ago immediately after a conversation, I should like to present the pieces of information in their original sequence. I hope I will be successful in showing that every single piece of information is structurally a component of a material-gestalt and cannot have gotten into the interview haphazardly. In its exact form, my intention can be carried out only on the basis of a verbatim protocol, which at this time is not yet at my disposal. That is why I intend to show by means of a single example what my own personal experience has confirmed for me again and again, ever since I have been working with this technique.

The patient, in contrast to our other patients, was an "elderly woman," although despite her white hair she looked younger and still gave the impression of being very vigorous and lively. I purposely emphasize her age because the entire conversation turned around an explanation of her personal past by which the patient still felt herself troubled. Despite her conscious motive of putting herself at the present time into a confrontation in the form of a treatment, all I was seeking was a reconciliation on her part with her personal fate. Her decision regarding treatment was solved for her by a chronic physical illness, the psychic genesis of which she believed she had recognized after having recently read a particular book. The distance from the past gave the conversation a certain lightness of tone and at many points brought out a gentle smile at the strange mistakes that human beings can make. At this point I should like to depart from the scenic element of this interview, which clearly begins to make itself felt, and—in line with my intention—let the temperate material have its say:

She is the classical schoolteacher type, dressed in a suit, her hair combed straight back from her forehead and fastened in a bun at the back, and wearing horn-rimmed spectacles. Her stern features are, however, made gentle by a sweet smile which makes her attractive and lends her a girlish charm. As she opens the conversation with the remark that, on the basis of what she has learned from the aforementioned book, she would like a confrontation with herself, I become frightened at the tone of her voice, from which one recognizes that she is in the habit of keeping many children under strict discipline and in good order. The patient is the oldest of seven children, but because of having been delicate and having had many childhood diseases, she was particularly spared, in contrast to her next-younger sister, who was brought up by her parents to perform all sorts of work. The father was a teacher by profession. He saw to it that all the children in the family did their share of work. The patient alone enjoyed an exceptional position.

At this moment I made my first remark by summarizing her intention of confronting her chronic illness and its psychic background with something like this: "Apparently you have always had to struggle very hard against this possibility of obtaining special privileges with the help of your illness, and being spared." The patient confirms this remark that puts into words the exact opposite of the external impression she makes on me, by declaring that she had always been harsh with herself and that she had never given in to tendencies to spoil her. That probably her chronic illness was the expression of these secret and combated wishes. That her parents had, to be sure, for this reason treated her very considerately as a child, but that any consideration like this had later, especially in her professional career, never again been given her. On the contrary, in order finally to get rid of this illness she had submitted to several operations, but these had never been successful, and even to this day she had to endure these ills.

From these data, we put together the first section of the gestalt. The patient had identified with her father in looks, bearing, and profession, but she is even stricter against a soft and perhaps maidenly side in herself than her father used to be. This rejected part of her personality lets itself be heard from in her illness, and this is what she has to be troubled about. Probably her own insight through her reading of the book had made headway up to this point.

The patient now continues that besides suffering from this chronic illness she suffers occasionally from depression. She declares at once, in connection with this, that these come from her mother, for many relatives on the mother's side of the family had suffered from depression, and some had even made suicide attempts. I do not go directly into this change from the protective fatherly aspect to the dangerous motherly feminine one, but I show the patient my understanding of it: that even in her privileged position as a pampered child she had felt very lonely and isolated and perhaps had been fearful that things might happen to her as they had to the mother's relatives.

While this is going on I find myself thinking that what is delicate and maidenly in this patient is very much endangered. The patient now corrects herself by saying that perhaps she has not been so hard on herself, for although in school she was always afraid of failure, yet her profession also gave her a great deal of pleasure and she put a lot of thought into establishing an understanding with the children and creating an atmosphere in which learning would be fun for the children. While she is saying these things, there comes over her face again that tender, likable smile, which lets me get a glimpse of how far she has become reconciled with her fate and how she no longer feels lonely among these children. The identification with the father, as difficult as it is for her, protects her when she is with the children from dangerous loneliness, which is bound up with the motherly feminine aspect.

While I am thinking this over, I ask the patient what sort of a life she has had. This question, which is kept indeterminant, is designed to enrich by concrete facts from her life the unconscious gestalt that has been arrived at up to this point (identification with the father and avoidance of involvement in her feminine role). Willingly she replies to my question and, to begin with, tells me that as a young girl she had become acquainted with a young man who lived far away. They corresponded a good deal with one another and planned on getting married. In this phase of the relationship, it occurred to her to send her friend a photograph of herself. From that moment on, she never heard a word from him again. Later she became aware that this picture had been taken when she was in one of her depressive phases. She could no longer understand how she had ever come to send him just this very picture and is even today still convinced that on the basis of the impression created by this picture, the friend had withdrawn. After a short pause, however, she continues thoughtfully that it might perhaps also have been the fear of having a child, for an illegitimate child at that time would have been an insoluble problem. Which I supplement by saying, "And that's also why you didn't have any sexual relations with him." "No, of course not," she immediately answers. Then she adds that she had never in her life had any intimate contact with a man.

Our picture is now rounded out: As a girl she cannot and may not have any contact with a man because she might have a child and in her despair would have to commit suicide, as frequently happened in those days. The feminine aspect, corresponding to our earlier statement concerning structure, remains the threatening element which is not permitted to become a reality and has got to be suppressed with the help of the male identification. The identification with the female aspect still always calls forth depression, isolation, and notions of suicide, but yet has been combined with a new theme. The element that has conjured up the danger is no longer the pampered and privileged position that is connected with the female aspect, but the threat of female sexuality through an illegitimate child.

In order to make understandable the gestalt that has been developed in its infantile unconscious connotation up to this point, we offer a genetic connection from our experience. We have to assume that as a little girl the patient was disturbed by the unconscious wish to have a baby from her father, like her mother did; for she had lived through six pregnancies of her mother's. This prevalent infantile wish was her real problem, and not the fantasized danger of becoming pregnant through her friend, with whom she had no sexual contact for this reason. The experience with the friend, in the succession of information provided in the interview, takes the place of the unmentionable infantile unconscious fantasy (cover memory) and reveals to us the central anxiety of her infantile neurosis. We fill in the gaps from data that are already known. Because of this anxiety, she broke off the beginning of her feminine relationship to her father, by getting from him, with the help of her depression and her need for being pampered, a special privileged position of a different kind. We may be sure that she did not confront her father in the guise of a coquette and as though she were in love, as we can so frequently observe in young daughters. This privileged position did not affect her relationship to her mother. Nonetheless, the mother remained latent in the role of the powerful rival because, behind the privileged condition occasioned by her illness, the unconscious fantasy lay in wait for the realization of her wish. To strengthen the privileged position in her relation to the father, the patient had later identified with him and thereby in a noninsidious way had again come closer to him. The only relationship with a man in her life upset her mental equilibrium. Following the pattern of the first love relationship with the father, the equilibrium was ended with the help of her sacrificing her disturbed feminine picture.

Let us return to the interview situation and ask ourselves, at the sight of the likable girlish smile on her otherwise very serious features, how the patient succeeded in preserving this feminine trait. In its content it embodies the innocent maiden.

In the actual conversation situation with the "elderly lady," this smile takes on a reconciliatory character, as though, even in her life, she had not wholly relinquished the realization of her feminine wishes.

To these reflections the patient gives a satisfactory reply with her next information. The successive data, accordingly, clearly and recognizably follow out the principle of relevancy. The patient is busy with the continuation of her life history and has no idea that the sequence of her remarks gains in significance because of our preunderstanding. After this disappointment with the young man, she devoted herself completely to preparations for her profession; but after the war she returned to her parents' home. There she continued to live with her parents and the younger sister nearest to her in age; the other siblings had already left home. When the parents took the illegitimate child of one of her sisters to live with them, she personally

cared devotedly for this child and saw to it that at the age
of ten the boy was sent to boarding school. After he
finished school—the parents had died in the meantime, and
the two sisters had taken over the house—the sisters took
the boy in to live with them and did all they could to give
him a real home. The patient believes that the boy had
"really gotten attached" to them. Now he had to be out of
the country a good deal, he made use of every opportunity
to visit her and her sister. "So you did at any rate understand how to bring up your 'own child' and open up unattainable facets of life for yourself," I suggest to her as
something to think about. In reply she merely smiles and
remains silent.

This comfortable agreement between us gives me the
courage to pose a question which, for no known reason,
occurs to me at this moment: "Haven't you ever in your life
suffered from the fact that, in this solution, you had to
remain physically unsatisfied?" Freely she admits that she
had masturbated from her childhood on until she was
grown—but always with a great sense of guilt and a feeling
of having committed a sin. Actually she had had to succumb, more as if it had been under the compulsion of the
physical urge. That sounds, considering the distance from
the past, perfectly natural. That is why I am the more
amazed when the patient, after a pause, says that even now
it occasionally happens that she feels such a passing urge.
At these words, a faint blush spreads over her face. She has
thus, until the present day, actually remained virginal, the
little girl with the likable smile, and the little girl who is
ashamed of her sexual desires. The contrast between her
sternness and the maidenly smiles has now given way to
maidenly blushing for shame. The fought-off maidenly/
womanly position has become the center of the conversation.

Although there now comes to light in the conversation
situation something very tender, feminine, which acts

touchingly lost rather than painful, the patient continues to convince me that in her masculine identification with her father, she has not only succeeded (without sexuality) in bringing up a child "of her own" but in addition (without sexuality) in having a "happy marriage." She is living, as has been stated, alone with her sister. The latter keeps house and looks after her at least as well as her mother looked after her father. The patient is busy with her teaching profession and earns the money for both of them. The sister often bemoans the fact that she has no money of her own at her disposal, although the two of them share the earnings. The patient goes into detail in her description of their joint problems until I can point out to her that both of them have the typical marriage conflicts that people have nowadays. Through her own descriptions she becomes increasingly aware that she is living with her sister in a "marriage community," and she recalls that she must dimly have felt something like this, for she had often jestingly said to her sister that they were married to one another. Thus the "son" comes to visit his "parents," gets spoiled and pampered by them, and when he leaves they are left at home alone like an elderly married couple whose child is grown. Suddenly the patient understands why she had often been afraid that she would not be able to cope with her school duties any longer, and she recognizes also that she, in her masculine identification, despite the many successful compensations, had always demanded too much of herself and had left something else stunted and undeveloped.

As she was about to leave, she declared that she now had a great deal to think about, and I believe that she realized that that, too, would have to remain as a compensation because a fundamental change in her unusual fate was no longer possible. This solution of her problem was not the worst possible one, even though, to be sure, it had to be purchased at the cost of a chronic physical illness and occasional depressions.

Chapter 8

THE AFTEREFFECTS OF THE CONVERSATION SITUATION

The dynamics of the scene in the conversation situation, true to their nature, provide for the further relationship to the interviewer or a reminder of him by a personal note. The patient, who according to his wishes and fantasies has at long last found in the interviewer the understanding he has always wanted, will strive for a continuation of the contact, at least will think of the interviewer with gratitude and high regard. All the possible relationship constellations come to be experienced in this way. We do not want to speak of such positive results of the interview in this connection, although they further the contact and also the patient's readiness for treatment in a way that we are glad to see. Our preferred interest has got to center on the negative results, because these work in opposition to the goal of the initial interview.

All patients who suffer from obvious symptoms of mental or psychic illness feel themselves to be the victims of alien, unconscious forces, even though they have already acquired the knowledge that these have something to do with their own person. The forces remain "ego-alien," as we call it. We have heard that the patients set the stage for a resistance against directing these unconscious proceedings onto themselves and accepting them into consciousness. This ability to keep certain mental contents away from consciousness provides a natural defense for the personality, even when this has disturbing and pathological manifestations as a result. Apparently in many respects illness represents the lesser evil—as opposed to the danger of doubting oneself in the face of the ideas and the ideal formations which one has acquired about oneself. Every confrontation with the unconscious heightens either the resistance or else has traumatic results, which work out as being offended, coupled with a reproach against the interviewer. This unambiguous fact is the reason why psychotherapeutic treatments require long periods of time, because the enlargement of consciousness with respect to mental or psychic illness makes its way along many bypaths and resistance maneuvers.

That is why the interviewer finds himself in a definite dilemma. If he does not get the patient to participate in getting to know the backgrounds of his own disturbance and looks upon him merely as a source of information, the interviewer's theories concerning the illness will remain incomplete and often unconvincing, as we have already suggested. Besides, the interviewer will not learn anything about whether the patient is really suitable for conversation treatment, with what particular personality-bound resistances he will have to reckon, and how these are related to the patient's disturbance. Under these circumstances, the prognosis and the indication for psychotherapeutic treatment can be made only when there is a working together of clinical experience and diagnosis without any consideration of the individual variant of what is taking place in the disturbance of this particular patient. Added to this is the fact that today's concept system with respect to diagnosis is still not obligatory. That is why the interviewer must count on a high quota of mistakes and disappointments, which one can no longer be responsible for when the patient is not the only one to assume the financial responsibility—when the public, for example, an insurance company, is burdened with it.

If, on the other hand, the interviewer uses the conversation situation as a psychotherapeutic test and involves the patient insofar as the situation permits, then he has got to count on resistance which, after the conversation, often manifests itself as being offended, and, in addition, also runs the danger of being drawn into the whirlpool of a dynamic directed against him, even though he thereby comes face to face with something of the patient's capacity for cooperation and of his specific dynamics. In my work on the interview in 1967 (11) I described a woman patient, who consciously was exceedingly glad to come for a second interview, but who unconsciously gave me to understand that she had experienced the first interview under the slogan, "A man did something terrible to me." In accord with this formula, she made her husband responsible for her illness, and beyond that, expressed a dream theory as to the source of her suffering. She entertained the fixed notion that she could be relieved of her illness if in a dream one were able to find out what this frightful traumatic event was that she imagined. In this patient the individual unconscious dynamics of the scene had further covered over the feeling of being offended and called forth an unconscious conflict with the interviewer which did not in any way dim the external relationship with him, and not even the memory of him.

M. and E. Balint in 1961 in their book (12) upheld the same point of view:

The interviews at the psychiatrist's, also the test session, are unexpected events and can therefore, in contrast to a long-er-lasting treatment, have a traumatic effect. The shock experienced in the interview can have a therapeutic effect, especially if it occurs in an ordinary relationship, created by the physician and accepted by the patient.

In this connection, I should like to quote an example. One evening a foreigner, a woman who was traveling through Germany, urgently demanded a talk with me. She was in a definite panic situation. The first impression of her personality and the threatening internal crisis led me to conduct a straightforward conversation with her and, insofar as it was in any way possible, to give her the opportunity to participate in my findings. I did not attempt to quiet her down but was completely open, although I limited myself strictly to the manifestations resulting from our conversation situation. The patient grew outwardly calmer during our conversation but continued on her journey—according to my judgment—inwardly in a turmoil.

Fully half a year later, she wrote me a letter, a few typical passages of which I should like to quote:

I have a bad conscience that I am thanking you only today. I have made four previous attempts to do do, but I tore all of them up. Today I can smile about it. But I must say you were really very hard on me. Fear and dismay about it are in my bones to this very day. . . . What helped me the most was the temperate way in which you presented reality. It is amazing what we make of a situation when our emotions are involved. Beyond that, you gave me the best advice that I have received in my whole life. That advice in the past five months actually led me to test myself and almost tore me apart. You simply cannot conceive how I would have liked to ask you for advice sometimes despite all my fear of you —for one does not so easily lay aside the habits of a lifetime —but I now take pains to judge critically what I do in this respect. . . . Above all, I marvel at your knowledge of human beings. You were right in almost everything, and things did

turn out as you had told me they would . . . I am in good
shape.

In a few lines I thanked her for this letter and again,
half a year later, I had further news:

Your letter was amazing to me insofar as it had never entered my mind that the one who gives advice also plays a part
in the conversation. By rights I ought to know that about
myself. In the relationship of psychiatrist to patient another
item is added: shame. One lays bare one's inmost soul, then,
when the excitement has died down, anger and shame begin
to appear at having so far "exposed" oneself. Harsh criticism is hard to bear, particularly when it hits the nail on the
head. Criticism can cause great turmoil—that I now know
about myself. I took long enough before I had once again
regained my equilibrium sufficiently to be able honestly to
be grateful. How much I am taking to heart everything that
I learned from you I will explain at once. . . .

There followed a very detailed description of two events
which now made it possible for her to look back on her
former attitude critically and to put considerable distance
between it and herself.

Thus an interview conversation that lasts barely an
hour can have an aftereffect, if what is unusual in the situation is brought out into the open. This example of an
emergency situation, surely not worth being copied,
teaches us as an extreme case what dangerous processes
can be set in motion in an initial interview, what real results
they can have in a personality less capable of insight and
less stable in personality, and with what circumspection we
must make use of this instrument. This experience also
brings home to us a graduated differentiation of the initial
interview techniques from a purely diagnostic, a therapeutic, and an emergency viewpoint—techniques with which
we will be further concerned.

In connection with our present theme, I should like to

explain somewhat more fully the nature of aftereffects. In doing so I shall leave the actual scenic element out of the picture, to take up instead the more generally legitimate instances with which we have to deal quite independently of the scenic dynamics.

The remarks in the letter concerning my advice and my supposed knowledge of human beings which had turned out to be so valuable refer to an insight which, in this externally altogether quiet but very frank conversation, I had gained from her illness situation in conformity with the actual scene: That because of her attitude of great dependence, she would again and again have to mix into the affairs of others and would thereby get into a situation of helplessness. This formulation certainly sounds very banal to an outsider, superficial, and with rather little meaning. Her present hitting of the bull's-eye is due in no way to my knowledge of human beings but rather to the circumstance that I evidently was able to put her in touch with the scenic element of the situation. Through this, the patient's resistance lost its momentary force, and she was able to perceive her problems, which she fully understood only much later through her actual life circumstances. From my formulation she deduced the advice for herself: "Don't keep mixing into other people's affairs, but prove to yourself that you can be independent and on your own." Following this advice—which, as already stated, the patient had given herself —confronted her with completely new life experiences. It took the latter to help her to the realization of how great her dependence had actually been previously, and in what great helplessness her tendency to mix into other people's affairs had continually placed her. She herself writes; "That advice led me to test myself." Accordingly, she had to struggle against herself, against her earlier personality stance. "One doesn't so easily cast aside the habits of a lifetime," even if—we must now add—helplessness and panic are its results. In this case, illness appears to be the lesser evil.

Despite her insight into the rightness of and justification for what I did, the patient in her ambivalent emotional state had to pass through a pronounced negative reaction towards me. "Fear and dismay to this day still sit in my bones." The comparison between my formulation, and according to her, the theme-centered conversation with its negative reaction extending over the span of half a year, permits of no doubt that the offense arises from an inner source in the patient. In her second letter, the patient writes that she could express her thanks to me only after she once again had regained her equilibrium. This sentence should be taken literally. The conversation situation with me had shaken her out of her psychic equilibrium, had appreciably destroyed previous harmony, and had forced her to put herself in the way of new experiences with the changes in her life. In her test she was already struggling with herself. In the second letter, a year later, she corrected her opinion of me further: "It would never have entered my mind that the one who gives advice also has a part to play in a conversation." The interviewer was transformed for her from a harshly critical phantom into a human being. Only under this condition could the patient explain what had occurred: "One lays bare one's innermost soul. Once the excitement has died down, anger and shame appear at one's having so far exposed oneself." In this ambivalent attitude one again senses a reproach: "Criticism is hard to bear, criticism can cause a great turmoil, that is something I now know myself." Once again, on the basis of the conclusion, the suspicion exists that the patient is pushing off her criticism of herself onto the interviewer and is relieving herself of the burden at his expense. Such behavior seems thoroughly justified, as it was the interviewer who had been the one to introduce this process, albeit with the patient's participation and agreement. He, without any equivocation, bears the responsibility for such an aftereffect of the conversation. Without this participation it would not have taken place—at all events, not in this dramatic form.

The patient brought out the evidence of the formulation to protect her resistance, and this had left her the possibility of being unburdened only by abreacting her anger onto the interviewer. In place of the resistance, an aggression is released which accompanies the new construction of the psychic equilibrium and visibly dies down after a new harmony has been reached. "Today I smile at it."

No thoughtful interviewer will set such a dangerous process in motion without urgent need. The process is, in the long run, inescapably necessary for a cure; but it can act as a sudden shock or, in the presence of the patient's acute anxiety, can appreciably heighten his or her protective resistance.

As a consequence of the interview technique, there arises the task of releasing the explosive power potential, in accordance with the patient's personality, without endangering the goal of the interview and falling back onto the simple collection of data. The course of the conversation situation itself, and with it the observation of the patient's reactions, are by no means a certain criterion. From our patient we have learned that the negative reaction after a latency period appears as soon as the excitement has died down and the insights that have been gained give notice of their demands.

This matter of excitement is obviously of the utmost importance. We encountered it frequently in the seminars with our practicing physicians, who come upon their patients in an acute phase much more frequently than we psychotherapists do. In this state of suffering the patients are much more honest with themselves, and accordingly also approachable for suitable interpretation. Under these circumstances, the interpretation can perceive a therapeutic opportunity, but it can also provide the occasion for taking offense in a massive way. I described such a case in my work (13), one in which the physician missed his opportunity, and in a misunderstood identification with the psychotherapist, after the dying down of the acute phase of the illness, came upon a phase of psychic resistance which, on the basis of his training, he was not able to deal with. In the acute condition of excitement caused by the illness, the patient is less well protected by his resistance, which is bound to his personality. This fact ought to warn us to practice the utmost care, even when in an emergency situation we would like to perceive a chance to be helpful. The patient who in a prearranged interview meets us quietly with his full-blown resistance in force is in much less danger.

Many other factors play a part in the negative aftereffects. Thus, for example, the fully enlightened patient who seeks the interview with false notions is either not at all reachable or else surprisingly capable of being traumatized. Later, because of a lack of insight, he will not possess the ability to meet head-on his tendency to reproach the interviewer, and to overcome his ambivalence, the way the woman patient we have been concerned with did—albeit after a surprisingly long interval—succeed in doing.

Chapter 9

THE INTERVIEW AS A THRESHOLD SITUATION

At one time (14) we chose the word *Grenzsituation* (threshold situation), in lieu of a more descriptive concept, to characterize the intermingling of the various information processes at a particular point in time. Objective, subjective, and situational data, in certain phases of the conversation situation assume an unwarranted importance as testimony. W. Schraml designates the critical point of such a phase as a threshold. In his example (page 8), it took 25 minutes after the most careful unwinding of objective data before the threshold was reached at which a dynamic information-gestalt constituted the main element of the self-testimony, and this under the heading of, "It is hard to live with a person who is that much of a perfectionist." In conjunction with the data on the family conflict, the interviewer was able to understand, on the basis of a passing identification with the relatives, what elements this conflict released and could, accordingly, verbalize it in the form of a question. The patient's immediate reaction confirmed, as evidence he had himself experienced, the correct understanding of the information which had been unconsciously presented, exposed the dynamic situation process, and later provided the important information that he could up to a certain point, lay aside his apparently rigid stereotype and was capable of gaining insights.

One sees clearly how at this point in the conversation the progressing material-gestalt, the dynamics of the scene, and the aftereffect of an interpretation in the form of a question run together into new information. This phenomenon of the initial interview we designate as the threshold situation. In doing this one has to realize that the patient as well as the interviewer produces accomplishments in the way of communication and must display capacities for perception before a single information-gestalt comes into being. A large part of these communication processes proceed preconsciously; that is, they are not directly accessible to consciousness. Today we are still far from being able to grasp these proceedings fully and to explore them. Therein apparently lies one of the reasons why subjective and situational factors are still observed with the greatest reserve, although there is no sensible argument in psychotherapy for the fact that objective data provide more reliable information than do other kinds. Our higher education in science innoculates us with a relentless harshness to the effect that only such information regarding illness is to be regarded as reliable as is obtained on the basis of objective criteria and can be checked.

In this training, however, we are not candidly informed that a high price has to be paid for this objectivity, for the situations are too narrowly limited to the information levels that, according to the state of the science, still appear capable of being controlled. As correct as such a procedure is in the experimental sense, because it permits of objective checking, we must not hide the fact that man's limited knowledge alone justifies this protective measure. This limitation grows into a senseless prejudice where phenomena have to be observed and judged, in which the objective perception level is simply inadequate. In a crude comparison this attitude would mean that the phenomena that one makes out through a telescope or a microscope are not on a par with objective criteria, since one cannot reproduce them with the ordinary means at one's disposal. The only one who can confirm them is he who turns to the same instrument, and who knows how to manipulate it. Today no one would seriously cast doubts on the scientific value of such an instrument. At the time of its invention, to be sure, such a prejudice was frequently uttered. Now one knows the laws governing a microscope or a telescope, and that is the determining viewpoint. Today we know the laws of subjective and situational perception in only a very limited way, and that is why we tend to deny the results gained with other help, instead of admitting our ignorance. Doubtless phenomena do exist that we are able to observe with their help. First of all, laws do not as yet allow themselves to be as precisely determined as a strict scientific viewpoint demands.

Psychotherapy shares this fate with its sister science, medicine, in which the unsystematic observance of strongly empirical and perceptional-theoretical research hurried on ahead, because the healing of those who were suffering permitted of no other choice. Medicine, too, has had to work its way through a thicket of magic ways of thinking, and science as it advanced has confirmed a good deal that earlier had brought success through intuitive application, and had disclosed a good deal to be charlatanry. Today this particular development is by no means ended.

They do not admit it, but many experienced physicians permit themselves to be guided by the clinical look; many psychiatrists, by the so-called praecox-feeling. Such a method of perception ought to be rejected as unscientific and discarded, since nobody knows how it came into being and from whence it draws its assurance of hitting the bull's-eye. In these two disciplines that deal exclusively with human beings, the art of individual treatment still takes on a certain precedence over the scientific viewpoint. More recent investigations in various research directions are engaged in the scientific comprehension of creative thinking; here they stumble upon that unknown region of subjective perception. It is to be hoped that in the course of time they will provide further clarifications. In psychotherapy, too, this perception instrument is sought after by psychoanalysts, since psychoanalytical ego psychology has moved into the center of interest. The concept of "empathy" threatens to become a slogan. It makes the point that by way of empathetic understanding, what is alien can be recognized. Mothers develop this particular empathetic capacity so that they may understand the needs of their children that are essential for life. In rare instances people with severe mental illnesses, who are distinguished by their heightened dependence on others, possess the specific sensibility of understanding the unconscious processes in others. In group psychotherapy this capacity is termed "radar-function."

With this short discourse, I should like to point out that the critical attitude toward the utilization of subjective and situational data—insofar as it is still justified today—should not be allowed to lead to doing away with such data as unimportant, thereby robbing itself of very decided possibilities for knowledge. Criticism should rather spur us on to do more intensive research on the instruments of subjective perception. From the more recent history of psychotherapy we can learn how apparently objective criticism is influenced by the spirit of the times and how it becomes hardened into prejudices. The critics at the outset got hot and bothered by Freud's theory of sexuality; later, they tried to deny the discovery of the unconscious. These arguments nowadays scarcely draw anyone into serious polemics anymore, so critics take their flight into the accusation that we are unscientific. In doing so, they overlook the fact that modern psychotherapy is working out new fundamentals in the science of man. Modern psychotherapy in no way questions the principles of science; at all events, it calls forth a new way of thinking about the theory of science (15).

Inappropriate criticism can unnecessarily block research in this enormously important field and push the gifted new generation of scientists off into more attractive disciplines. With the frighteningly backward situation of psychotherapy as opposed to the tremendous forward leap of other scientific fields, we can no longer afford such a development. We hold fast to the following: Today the psychotherapist is working with a number of still partly unresearched perception functions. They appear in the interview in various phases during the course of the conversation and, in very painstaking and demanding training, are completed as far as the state of today's perceptions permits. In the case of the woman patient who lit her own cigarette, the significance of the scenic testimony was understood at the very beginning of the interview, but the incorporation of this information and its complete understanding came about only later with the appearance of the threshold situation, and with the help of other data. The so-called threshold situation, in which a number of methods of perception are integrated, can become evident at any time and as a surprise. The various methods of perception are coupled with processes that play an outstanding role in psychotherapy and might at least be mentioned by name, although a discussion of them actually belongs in the field of the technique of psychoanalysis: transference, countertransference, therapeutic ego-splitting, empathy, defense mechanisms, temporary identification, and regression in the service of the ego.

Suppose we go back once again to the example of the microscope. It does not suffice to know precisely the laws controlling the instrument in order to be able to make out the finer distinctions of the same substrata. What is determining for both research and practice, beyond that ability is the capacity to be able to interpret correctly what has been perceived. Not always does the stronger lens provide a more exact view—for it goes hand in hand with a diminution in the field of vision, and under certain circumstances with a lessening of the view as a whole. In general the sharply focused picture is so typical that the experienced person can make the diagnosis down to the smallest detail. Often, however, the picture is capable of many meanings, so that macroscopic findings have to be included in order that the material can be unequivocally identified. The same thing holds in psychotherapy. Accordingly the threshold situation is to be understood as the strongest magnification.

From this comparison we can draw two further important viewpoints for dealing with threshold situations. First, the undeniable but frequently overlooked fact is that knowledge and experience are an integral part of interpretation. Only someone who knows the important connections, who studies them time and time again and has gained experience in dealing with them, can correctly interpret sharply focused details—and, as already stated, not even that, every time. Frequently, even the experienced person recognizes only the significance and requires further data in order to be able correctly to incorporate the detail into the larger connections and by so doing to succeed in interpreting them in the right way. The first viewpoint that sounds obvious represents more of a warning, because in no other field is so much sinning done in good faith as in that of psychotherapy, in the notion that with one's own experience, a portion of sound common sense, and personal intuition, a good deal could be attained; specialized knowledge and long years of professional experience may be underestimated. The second viewpoint touches upon our particular theme.

On purely didactic grounds, we started from the conversation interview and have examined the information processes that are connected with it, but these have—I should like to call it—a merely focal character. For, with the help of this optical instrument, we focus on the texture that is very differentiated but yet limited to only one particular situation, that has become structured with one particular interviewer in this one-time situation. From our experience we know that the conversation situations can run a completely different course with a different interviewer. Sometimes as a stimulus for this it suffices to have an interviewer of the opposite sex. We have a good deal of elbowroom in our experience, because in our set-up almost every single patient is seen in two situations, an interview and a psychological test, and in the accompanying general conversation, the information obtained in both situations are compared. K. Lickint (16) has recently shown, in an impressive study, that even the same interviewer, if he has different expectations as to what he will hear, receives completely different information. This easy variability of the information picture corresponds somewhat to the lively change in expression of an externally unified organ that within itself contains many functional systems, each with its own structure, which can give rise to mistakes when there is isolated observation under great magnification, if one does not know the specificity of their all belonging to this organ together.

With our interview procedure as it has been presented up to this point, we thus arrive at a very precise assertion —but one, nonetheless, applicable only to this specific situation. This procedure owes its precision to the step-by-step clarification of the interpretation connections, with the patient's participation (subjective data). In many cases the structure of these focal diagnoses is already to typical that the experienced person can open up the entire picture of the illness and its potentiality. In other cases, the study of the processes of the illness must be continued by other means. For this purpose information is utilized which, in part, has been withdrawn from the work done up to this point; in part, it must be inquired about later (objective data). One has to know at what point in the conversation situation one can ask questions about data and when one cannot. There is a difference whether it is at the beginning or the end of the interview, outside of a dynamically colored scene, that one gathers information about siblings and the patient's position in the family—as in our example of the patient with the dark-skinned child—or lets the existence of a younger brother be confirmed at a specific point of time. In the first case, *we* try to give a meaning to the collected information in connection with the dynamic scene, where our general experience guides us (data exposure by the interviewer). In this procedure we practice a certain holding back, because all data primarily can be interpreted in many ways. In the second case we receive some information, the meaning of which has already been set forth and confirmed by the *patient* (data exposure by the patient).

Beyond the understanding of the threshold situation, we require further information, outside of the situation with the patient, for a second working through. In many institutions the patients are examined by a second person according to a carefully prepared list of questions. Understandably it is annoying if during this later, secondary comprehensive reworking of the material one stumbles upon an important question and then finds that one has not gotten any information on, for example, what the father's profession was.

Data that lie outside the scenic working through (threshold situation) are collected and then serve to provide a broader understanding of the patient's entire personality, a sort of postconstruction of the multifacetedness of the various spheres of his personality. The postconstruction embraces specifically the portions of his personality which could not become manifest in the conversation situation. The careful interpretation of this information is based, in the patient's absence, solely on the knowledge and clinical experience of the interviewer himself, or of another person knowledgeable in the field, but can now be called upon for a reconstruction of objective explanations beyond the meaning which the patient lends to it in his subjective attitude. These presuppose professional understanding which the patient, once again, does not possess. The secondary working over of the material is unreliable for research purposes, for reexamination of personality concepts, and for theoretical prognostications, and is taken care of in exemplary fashion in the "Hampshire Diagnostic Profile"(17). For these purposes the collection of data cannot be accurate enough, a demand which in a conversation situation can scarcely be realized by the interviewer. Either one must broaden the examination procedure or introduce a documentation of the data which is set up on the basis of well-considered viewpoints. With the unstoppable, all-prevailing forward thrust of computerization, a second method of optimal data documentation will become a reality one of these days and will somewhat lessen the interviewer's task in his complicated situation with the patient.

The further this secondary working over of the factual information advances, the more it is removed from the patient's individual picture, becomes an ideal type construct of his illness and its personality components, and makes him, for research purposes, comparable with other pictures of illness. For the purely clinical needs it is therefore important to maintain the contact with the interview scene or to retranslate the reconstruction scenically and to imagine oneself in live relationship models. These various techniques of using the material are not subject to any comparable utilization, but are to be distinguished strictly according to the sources of information, the instruments of the working over, and the goals that they serve. The strong emphasis on the conversation situation itself and the possibilities of its evaluation correspond to the routine requirements of psychotherapeutic practice and the opening up of a source of information which is very far from being exhausted and which confronts the thinking of the natural sciences with the greatest difficulties. The psychological interpretation of objective data is a procedure that in its diversity is well known from the literature. The threshold situation in the initial interview thus represents the dividing line at which the decision is made with respect to how far one can and will proceed with which source of information and what goal one will pursue in the interview: a purely diagnostic, therapeutic, emergency-therapeutic, or scientific-research one. The intensification of all these aspects of the initial interview is possible with the help of modern television transmissions. H. E. Richter (18) has systematically built up this procedure and created a new type of interview—that is, the "teaching," or rather the "learning," interview.

Chapter 10

THE DIAGNOSTIC INTERVIEW

Under the title "Der Psychoanalytische Befund" (19) I assembled the material of a threshold situation that might be briefly sketched as follows: The patient, referred to us by an institution, appeared accompanied by his wife, who sat patiently in the waiting room awaiting his return from the interview. He sat before me, a man with work-roughened hands, his figure hunched over, brooding dully, perspiring. He was silent and gave me time to observe him quietly and to let the picture he presented have its effect on me. After a while he began the conversation with a piece of scenic information. It let me recognize his intention, without any equivocation, of showing me the authenticity of his disturbance. "I'll have one of my fainting spells immediately if you light yourself a cigarette." At the same time he made moves to show me the black and blue spots that he had acquired in his last spells.

Consciously it was surely painful for the patient to be set down opposite a doctor—as had occurred so often—

who would not believe in his illness. Besides, he must have been afraid that, not recognizing his suffering, I would want him to do things which he, because of his illness, believed himself incapable of. It was obvious that anger and despair about his hopeless expectation were battling inside him.

If one observes what was taking place with the optics with which the unusual situation is usually looked at, then his remark takes on the character of an unconscious threat: Don't you dare light a cigarette!

The dynamic aspect of this warning lends the patient a threatening latent aggression. It is emphasized by his dully brooding manner, as though he were struggling against internal violent impulses—although consciously he presented himself as the victim of his disturbance, as if it were the unconsidered action of some other person. The subjective meaning of this scenic opening will become apparent for the sensitive person only in the later course of the conversation, together with the biographical data. Asked about the cause of death of his youngest sister, the patient recalls from his mother's report that the little girl had died in her crib when the oldest brother set fire to some straw in the room and then ran out of the room in horror at sight of the flames and smoke. Thus, the youngest child had been the victim of the oldest brother's unconsidered and dangerous action. The detailed circumstances were the same as those that the patient unconsciously had made known in the scenic structuring of the interview: "If you light yourself a cigarette, I'll have a fainting spell." The meaning of the second informational part of the scene, showing off the blue spots, becomes evident the moment the patient mentioned with emotion that his father, when angry, had often beaten him, and that he therefore had constantly run around with black and blue spots. The complete scenic information of the subjective laying bare of his illness reads: "I am the victim of dangerous, ill-considered, and wrathful impulses on the part of my oldest brother and father. You can convince yourself of the correctness of what I tell you by what you see."

The presumed latent aggressive element of the situation, the threatening mien against the interviewer which indicates the intrapsychic conflict, the fight against one's own violent impulses (identification with father and brother) also received confirmation from the biographical data. The fainting spells compelled the patient to give up his job as driver of a public transportation vehicle after a passenger had been killed, though it was not his fault. This "unpremeditated" violent deed stamped him as a "doer" (instead of a victim). Logically, he must now follow the fate of those whom he himself had unconsciously brought into the conversation as the external representations of violence. The patient, exactly like his father and his oldest brother, was prematurely pensioned off because of illness.

Up to this point, we have thrown light on the patient's illness, for which the doctors could never find any physical cause, as the expression of an actual intrapsychic conflict. This occurred exclusively with the help of the scenic information which the subjective meaning of his illness had revealed to us. We can now understand what anxieties the demand to return to his job must have awakened in him. This specific anxiety was dominant throughout the entire interview.

The clarification of the meaning connection of the symptom with the conflict concealed behind it is only the first step that we in general have to take in the diagnostic interview; for in regard to the indication attitude and prognosis attitude we have to know more about what kind of personality is embedding this illness, what capabilities the patient possesses, and with what structure-specific difficulties or resistances we have to reckon in the treatment. That is why in a second work session we complete our understanding of the scene connected with the symptom for the purpose of a diagnosis of the structure of the patient's personality. The intensive discussion of the diagnosis of the structure shows up difficulties in comprehension and makes a broadly laid out theoretical basic discussion desirable. That is why, to round out our example, I want to repeat some indications.

Our patient consciously experiences himself as a good person and can cite many examples to prove that he never purposely did anything bad. As a young man he traveled about as a musician, played for other people to dance to, but afterwards always had a drink and immediately went home; he never got into fights. In contrast, his father was definitely quick-tempered and uncontrolled, although his mother must have been a friendly person. Apparently the patient had early identified with the good mother and, correspondingly passive, experienced himself as the victim of the bad father and made every effort to keep out of his way. From these not-yet-evaluated pieces of information, one can round out the picture of the patient's personality beyond the actual conflict and come upon viewpoints that are structurally specific.

Besides, from his life data, we can read that the patient limits his life because of strong conscientious demands and suffers from strong unconscious guilt feelings which are attached to his "supposed murder." His imaginative world is filled with practical, everyday occurrences. As a conversational partner he remains dull, without insight, and anxiously avoids everything that could touch him emotionally, although in the scene that he unconsciously made up, he can make his conflict surprisingly transparent. This accomplishment of the scenic function of the ego apparently belongs to the organs of information that were developed early and remains even in less differentiated personalities. In some way the patient remains almost stubbornly attached to his own views and is not to be moved toward reflective thinking. His tendency toward passive withdrawal keeps the upper hand. That is why it is impossible to work on a problem with him to teach even minimal results. Outwardly willing to cooperate, he agrees to a second conversation, but after the interview he disappears into a hospital and never lets himself be heard from again. For understandable reasons he was, despite the distress of his suffering, in no way motivated for treatment and had come for the interview only on the instigation of the institution that had sent him.

At this point I should like to break off consideration of this particular case and take up the more general problems of the diagnostic interview. The patient's participation in the conversation, in consideration of the possible aftereffects, will be limited to regions that are absolutely essential for diagnostic understanding, setting up the indication, and the prognosis. The diagnostic interview should, therefore—to alter a well-known quotation of Freud's (20) —remain a standard activity that uses the smallest possible amounts of energy. The advice is especially to be taken to heart if one does not yet know whether the patient can be accepted for subsequent treatment.

The task of the diagnostic conversation is not completed with the demand for diagnostic clarity. The best diagnostic perceptions do not help the patient if they do not flow together into a concrete treatment plan that takes account of his internal and external reality. Beyond that, the patient must be motivated for treatment and prepared for it; without a properly understood cooperation, the prognosis remains in doubt, particularly in cases in which a referral to a colleague is unavoidable. Elsewhere I have already mentioned how specific resistances can block any diagnostic understanding as well as the mobilization of readiness for treatment. That makes me think of the many unproductive patients who, checkmated by such resistance, wear out the interviewer and externally call forth the impression that they are not interested in the conversation. The interviewer will in no way be spared getting at least as far in the resistance phenomena so that he can estimate what value they possess for the treatment and also can sound out whether behind them realms of the personality are alive which let a therapeutic intervention appear rewarding.

This second phase of the diagnostic interview has more of a psychotherapeutic character, although it considers itself exclusively as a preparation for treatment. J. V. Coleman pleads for it as follows: "To offer the treatment process by demonstrating it rather than explaining it, and to offer the patient the opportunity to take part in such a treatment experience" (21). Without pressing him or trying to persuade him, we ought to motivate him through the style of our conducting the conversation, so that he himself is in a position to reach the important decision for treatment. Under certain circumstances we provide sufficient elbowroom and offer ourselves for a second conversation, the initiative for the setting of which is left to the patient.

The separation of the diagnostic initial interviewing into two phases is done for teaching purposes that indicate centers of gravity for the tasks on hand. Actually, both goal settings run together from the very beginning of the conversation. With the technique advocated in this book, what happens at the beginning already contains both elements: the seeking after diagnostic clarity and the step-by-step participation of the patient in the perception process as a test experience. We thereby avoid the fault so frequently to be observed in practice, whereby an interviewer performs a good diagnostic function but thereafter does not really know what concretely to propose to the patient. Sometimes he has even neglected to find out whether the patient is interested in having treatment. In the course of the examinations at the Sigmund Freud Institute, a second conference is arranged for this purpose, in which what has been left out can be put in, while—in case it is necessary—an opportunity is once again provided in a test phase to ventilate plans for treatment and to find out about the patient's readiness for treatment. The technique of this part of the conversation aims to utilize the knowledge that has been gained in the interview for this special task, and under circumstances where it is necessary to make up for what has been missed by supplying from this material a passage of real resistance work with interpretations.

The work of preparation in the initial interview or in the second discussion must not be confused with the pre-discussion for the actual treatment in which the "rules of the game" for the psychotherapeutic procedure are amicably set forth. If the interviewer himself takes over the treatment, it is of course left open to him at what point in time he ends the preparation phase in order to discuss, at that or some other time, in a factual talk without therapeutic attitudes, the rules of the projected treatment, and to make them clear to the patient. This prediscussion is part of the treatment and primarily has nothing to do with the themes of the initial interview. Many authors do not conceptually separate these two procedures from each other sharply enough.

Chapter 11

THE THERAPEUTIC INTERVIEW

Adding the word "therapeutic" designates the setting of a goal for a limited therapeutic task, one that is commensurate with a conversation or with a few conversations. The therapeutic intention will in no way attempt to make the false demand of coming up with a psychotherapeutic procedure of its own. As we have already seen, the creation of a readiness for treatment under certain circumstances furthers a short passage of real psychotherapeutic resistance work, even if we understand preparation to mean only a projected treatment process. Even more important than the striving to win over the suitable patient is the change-over to a limited therapeutic goal-setting in patients who, to begin with, do not wish to have treatment or early prove themselves to be unsuited for treatment. In such instances, the talk more quickly turns into counseling, while the diagnostic aspect retires to the background.

I described a typical example of this in the chapter on the gestalt of the conversation situation Chapter 7. Here, because of the unchangeable life situation, the patient's age, and the distance from the residence, a treatment was scarcely to be considered. The task of this one-time counseling was shown during the conversation, as the patient gave me to understand that she felt disturbed by her past and let her determination show through, on the basis of her chronic physical illness, to engage in an inner confrontation with herself. This demand was almost touching in view of the absolute impossibility of changing her life in any decisive way. It did seem, however, to provide a sufficiently well-founded point of departure to impute to her our joint observation of the disturbing conflicts of her past, to reconcile her somewhat with her personal fate, and to help her to be able to enjoy life more. Such a modest goal gives the conversation a constructive meaning and leaves open the possibility of continuing this one-time therapeutic contact—in case it is necessary—in a loosely handled succession of conversations. With this suggestion I left her—but she never came back.

In contrast to this, the patient who "looked after herself" (from chapter 6, on the dynamics of the conversation situation) used the same suggestion and at intervals of several months appeared for a number of conversations. Unconsciously well motivated, she received from me the "nourishment" with which she supplied herself for months on end. The success of these few talks was striking, for the patient was able to manage herself in her marriage in a completely new way and could enjoy it happily, something she had thought was no longer possible. My technique was in no way designed to doubt her capacity for "looking after herself"; rather I counted on this capability, for the reason that the patient in the foreseeable future would have to rely on it. The theme of the threshold situation loosened the stereotype of self-sufficiency at any price sufficiently so that the patient could reserve it for those situations in which it was really called for. By doing so she could permit herself to be much less embarrassed than her unconscious distrust had permitted up to this time.

The information of the threshold situation, coming from subjective, objective, and situational sources, provides the structure of an actual surface for those momentary conversation periods. The sharply etched information gestalt either offers itself as the point of departure for a diagnostic understanding of the specific personality, or it represents the basis for psychotherapeutic counseling. In the latter instance, the art of the interviewer is measured by his handling it exhaustively but not beyond the limits set by this structure. The often banal-sounding formulation that the threshold situation should not be allowed to deceive us as to what highly specific and, under certain circumstances, even explosive, effect it can have. M. Balint's work group in London (22), following a similar view, has developed a short-term therapy which, in a limited number of hours, works exclusively on a single "focal" conflict that has been determined by the material obtained in the interview, and insofar as possible does not depart from it. The results of this research group underline the great significance of the initial interview, for the principle of this short-term therapy is based solely on its knowledge.

Besides the evaluation of criteria for the patient's suitability for such a limited treatment, it is definitely a matter of finding the right—and thus also the operationally effective—formulation of the "focus" which will become the bearer of this short segment of a conversation. One may not succumb to the mistaken notion that in this way a simple and easy-to-practice technique for short-term therapy has been inaugurated. Yet this principle is so convincing that in Germany it has served as godfather for the guidelines for insurance for psychotherapy (23, 24). It is derived wholly organically from our conceptions concerning the initial interview. Perhaps this form of therapy is destined to have a future, if it continues to be pursued on the basis of good criteria and with psychotherapeutic knowledge and skill.

Accordingly the task of counseling arises as an outgrowth from the course of the conversation and requires ability for quick reactions, a clear perspective, and the capacity to make judgments. The interviewer is completely left to his own devices. In the short-term therapy described above, on the other hand, a group of therapists generally is turned in as a team. The team views the material, ventilates the focus, tests it for its usefulness, and makes prognostications. Colleagues can accompany the one who is handling the patient in his work and in weekly group discussions, and can control him, counsel him, and be helpful in the understanding of the short-term therapy process. The clear didactic build-up of the short-term treatment field that can be seen as a whole makes focal therapy seem especially suitable for training purposes.

Much more demanding than the therapeutic counseling session is the emergency interview, for in it the interviewer works under high pressure and is left entirely to his own devices, with a great deal of responsibility. In the shortest possible time he must find diagnostic considerations, draw significant consequences from them, and arrange his treatment method in accordance with them. The main difference in all the rest of the conversation situations lies in the fact that the patient turns up in a state of acute suffering and is not, as is usually the case, shielded and protected by his mental or psychic defense mechanisms. There is a certain chance in this, but also a risk that is not to be underestimated. In chapter 8 on the aftereffects of the conversation situation, I sketched such a conversation.

Making the emergency therapy real to a greater extent presupposes great personal and financial possibilities which we do not have at our disposal, so that we ourselves could make only sporadic attempts at this form of interview. In America a project of this type was carried on over a period of several years, and its results were published in a book (25). Although the involvement of personnel was very considerable in view of our particular circumstances, the territory had to be limited in the course of this project because the continuous pressure on psychotherapists day and night raises demands to which an insitution cannot, under normal circumstances, accede for a prolonged period. Despite all the difficulties, the technique of the emergency interview remains of burning actual interest because it is asked for everywhere where there are people who are ready to help, in telephone counseling and other institutions that are constantly on call. Besides the technique of the conversation, in the emergency interview there are other naturally helpful measures that play an important part—such as medication, in-patient treatment, and opening up treatment channels in social work.

Chapter 12

TRAINING PROBLEMS

Learning the technique of the initial interview is an independent, even though frequently neglected, component of general psychotherapeutic training. As a rule the psychotherapist perfects the actual conversation technique only with practical experience, as one can determine from the protocols and reports of colleagues. The young psychotherapist frequently relies for too long a period on taking only those patients for personal treatment whom an older psychotherapy colleague has selected for him. The important pretest for those who in the later therapeutic process are directly involved is missing; and because of this, the quota of treatments broken off as unsatisfactory grows.

To enliven the activity for this neglected stepchild of psychotherapy, we at the Sigmund Freud Institute have instituted a permanent interview conference in which, on the basis of what appears in the protocol and in verbal reports the patient's personality structure, with its specific conflicts, defense structures and foreseeable developments under the conditions of the treatment process, are discussed. This common task has appreciably sharpened the consciousness for problems of diagnosis and has proved of value as a well-visited central point for training. On the other hand, it cannot be decided with certainty how far this occupation with the initial interview has importantly influenced the conversational technique of the individual.

Because of this we changed to the technique of carrying out teaching interviews through one-way mirrors. In America, the preliminary studies for this still controversial procedure were carried out some time ago (26). In the meantime, H. E. Richter (27) collected TV interviews and also published them. He points out especially what information is gained and the possibilities for diagnostic training and instructional help in the interview technique. In the work of his group one can see what research programs on the basis of existing interests, and what specific arrangements can be brought about by this method. Our special interest, the perception of scenic information, the working up of unconscious content and its integration into the personality structure, gain as evidence by the observation through the one-way mirror, because the scenic phenomena during direct and continuous observation can be controlled by several people.

To our very great surprise, we could definitely differentiate two perception processes in interviewers who were overwhelmingly empathetic in their work. On one such occasion, as observers behind the mirror, we had the impression that such an interviewer was very well able to grasp the complicated personality disturbances in their dynamic procedure-gestalt and also offered it to the patient in test formulations. We believed that we could observe precisely how the picture of this specific disturbance grew ever more sharply defined, because separate verbalizations of the interviewer took on an unusually clear-sighted validity. To us, too, the patient seemed to react visibly to these experiences with emotional phenomena. After the interview, this colleague—still entirely uninfluenced by our observations—reported his personal perceptions to us. To our great amazement we noted that he drew a picture of the patient quite different from that which we believed we had experienced in common, in the joint creation of a form, as between interviewer and patient. The interviewer based his argument on concrete portions of the material of the conversation and, in doing so, gave us to understand that he had formulated many of his remarks on the basis of constellations of external experiences based on what the patient had reported. Not until we directed his attention to the direct scenic givens, played back his own formulations on the soundtrack, and confronted him with the preconscious language that had been directed at the patient was it apparent to him.

The interviewer, in his empathy, had so exactly perceived the patient's unconscious personality picture and preconsciously worked through it, that one could from the soundtrack alone discern a clear conversation-gestalt. Consciously, he had put together the same information according to knowledge that he had at his command into a completely different personality picture from ours. In this impressive fashion, our old experience was confirmed: the interviewer always knows more about the patient than he is able to present. In this case, we naturally do not know how the final protocol would have looked without our influence. In all probability, one might assume, parts of the preconscious recognition processes observed by us to a greater or lesser degree would have flowed into the final evaluation at the second working through.

This tentative observation, which also agrees with psychoanalytical perception studies, has great consequences for the technique of training. We will participate in the cultivation and training of preconscious empathetical perception instrumentalities to a much greater extent and work for their integration into the theoretically acquired realms of knowledge.

Our interviewer had consciously directed his perception to the patient's information and had worked through this, commensurately with the extent of his training, toward his own knowledge. The observers not only looked at this objective information but also concentrated on the gestalt taking shape in the back-and-forth conversation, which in the increasing privacy of the language made itself known only now and yielded an understanding of the subjective meanings. At the beginning, the interviewer had not recognized how much he swung back and forth in his formulation about the language-gestalt, because he did not listen to what he himself was saying. We could easily recapture, with the aid of the soundtrack, the perception attitude that had been left out, and could point out to the interviewer the discrepancy between his thinking and his own verbal formulations.

In order to understand a patient's unconscious personality, the interviewer requires access to his own preconscious perception and thought processes, of which he is only in command when his consciousness participates in taking hold of them. *The secret of a comprehensive understanding in the initial interview is the participation of the interviewer's personality in the perception process.* The actively involved perception function goes in circles like a radar screen and takes information out of the objective data, the looks, and the behavior of the patient, the interviewer's emotional state and the reactions resulting from it, and finally from the observation of his own formulations, which arise from preconscious thought trailers. A good control for the integration of the various perception realms is the *Stimmigkeit* (agreement) in which the precision of the course of the conversation is mirrored. Only the contents formulated in this language serve as points-of-departure material for a secondary working over, for they contain in condensed form the unconscious dimension of the patient's personality. The reconstruction of the unconscious personality with its conflicts from the data alone remains speculative with many meanings, and can lead to errors, as we in our example were impressively able to coexperience it.

We return to a part of what we said at the beginning of this book: "The unusualness of the conversation situation comes about because an information that objectively appears meaningless, when it is connected with the situation, receives an unexpected significance."

From the interviewer we expect not only an understanding of the patient's words but must demand that he also be able to reconstruct the patient's specific personality from this language-gestalt. The interviewer is supposed to understand not only what the patient says but, over and above that, to be able to judge what the speaker's personality is. We try to identify the patient by his speech, which we get from him in the conversation, and then hear ourselves saying: "You have lost from your memory this connection which you already knew about, and I have restored it to you." We try to make a picture for ourselves of what sort of a personality this must be, which does not recognize its own mistakes but has to resort to receiving this knowledge back from someone else. We feel then that it must concern a person who is unable to maintain his own continuity and who has no capacity for recognizing something that is his own.

NOTES

CHAPTER 1

1. W. Schraml, "Ebenen des klinischen Interviews" [Stages of the Clinical Interview], *Person als Prozess* [Person as Process] (Bern/Stuttgart: Huber, 1968), p. 164.

CHAPTER 2

2. H. Argelander, "Der 'Patient' in der psychotherapeutischen Situation mit seinem behandelnden Arzt" [The "Patient" and His Attending Physician in the Psychoanalytical Situation], *Psyche* 20:1966, p. 926. In this work further references to the literature will be found, especially to the works of M. Balint.

3. A. Mitscherlich, *Krankheit als Konflkt, Studien zur psychosomatischen Medizin* [Illness as Conflict: Studies in Psychosomatic Medicine], 2 vols. (Suhrkamp Verlag, 1966, 1967).

4. M. Muck and J. Paál, "Kriterien der Behandelbarkeit und ihre Feststellung im Vorinterview" [Criteria of Treatability, and Its Determination in the Initial Interview] *Psyche* 22:1968, p. 770.

5. H. Argelander, "Das Erstinterview in der Psychotherapie" [The Initial Interview in Psychotherapy], *Psyche* 21:1967, p. 473.
6. L. Rosenkötter, Cl. de Boor, Z. Erdely, and J. Matthes, "Psychoanalytische Untersuchungen von Patientinnen mit funktioneller Amenorrhoe," [Psychoanalytic Investigations of Patients with Functional Amenorrhea], *Psyche* 22:1968, p. 838.

Chapter 3

7. H. Argelander: "Der 'Patient' in der psychotheupeutische Situation' [The "Patient" in the Psychotherapeutic Situation], *Psyche*: 1966, p. 926.

Chapter 5

8. H. Argelander, "Der psychoanalytische Dialog" [*The Psychoanalytic Dialogue*], *Psyche* 20:1968, p. 337.
9. A. Lorenzer, *Symbol und Verstehung im psychoanalytischen Prozess* [Symbol and Understanding in the Psychoanalytical Process], unpublished manuscript, pp. 245 ff., published 1970 in *Sprachzerstörung und Rekonstruktion* Suhskamp Verlag Frankfurt/M p. 194.
10. S. Freud, *Bruchstuck einer Hysterieanalyse* [Fragment from the Analysis of a Case of Hysteria], *Collected Works*, vol. 5, p. 282.

Chapter 8

11. H. Argelander, "Das Erstinterview in der Psychotherapie" p. 455.
12. M. and E. Balint, *Psychotherapeutische Techniken in der Medizin* [Psychotherapeutic Techniques in Medicine] (Bern/Stuttgart: Huber-Klett, 1961), p. 61.
13. H. Argelander, "Angewandte Psychoanalyse in der ärztlichen Praxis" [Applied Psychoanalysis in Medical Practice], *Jahrbuch der Psychoanalyse* Vol. 6: Huber, 1969.

Chapter 9

14. H. Argelander: "Das Erstinterview in der Psychotherapie," p. 429.

15. Cf. J. Habermass, *Erkenntnis und Interesse, Theorie 2* [Knowledge and Interest, Theory Vol. 2] (Suhrkamp, 1968).
16. K. Lickint, "Der Empfang des Patienten und das Erstinterview in der psychiatrischen Klinik" [The Reception of the Patient and the Initial Interview in the Psychiatric Clinic], *Der Nervenarzt* [The Psychiatrist] 39:1968, p. 451.
17. A. Freud, "Assessment of Childhood Disturbances," *Psychoanalytic Study of the Child* 17:1963, p. 149.
18. H. E. Richter, "Fernsehübertragung psychoanalytischer Interviews" [Television Psychoanalytic Interviews], *Psyche* 21:1967, p. 324.

CHAPTER 10

19. H. Argelander, "Der Psychoanalytische Befund" [Psychoanalytic Findings], *Psyche* 22:1968, p. 748.
20. S. Freud, *Ges. Werke* [Complete Works], vol. 15, p. 96.
21. J. V. Coleman, "The Initial Phase of Psychotherapy," *Bull. Menninger Clinic* 13/14; 1949/1950, p. 195.

CHAPTER 11

22. D. H. Malan, *Psychoanalytische Kurztherapie* [Short-Term Psychoanalytic Therapy], H. Huber (Bern/Stuttgart; E. Klett, 1965).
23. W. Loch, "Über theoretische Voraussetzungen einer psychoanalytischen Kurztherapie" [On Theoretical Suppositions for Short-Term Psychoanalytical Therapy], *Jahrbuch d. Psychoanalyse* Vol. 4: H. Huber, Bern/Stuttgart, 1967.
24. E. Mahler, "Zur Frage der Behandlungstechnik bei psychoanalytischer Kurztherapie" [On the Problem of Treatment Technique in Short-term Psychoanalysis], *Psyche* 23:1968, p. 823.
25. L. Bellak and L. Small, *Emergency Psychotherapy and Brief Psychotherapy* (New York: Grune & Stratton, 1965).

CHAPTER 12

26. M. Gill, R. Newman, and F. C. Redlich, *The Initial Interview in Psychiatric Practice* (New York: Internat. Univ. Press, 1954).

27. H. E. Richter, "Fernsehübertragung psychoanalytischer Interviews" [Television Broadcasting of Psychoanalytical Interviews], *Psyche* 21:1967, p. 324.

INDEX

Actual situation, 76, 108
Actual surface, 133
Aftereffects, 103, 107, 114, 127, 134

Basic information, 85
Basic rule for analysts, 94

Clinical evidence, 81
Common sense, 118
Compulsive-perfectionist character, 41
Concept of the initial interview, 25
Concrete treatment plan, 127
Conscious motivation, 40
Countertransference, 117

Demanding patient, 45
Development-gestalt, 34

Diagnostic interview, 123–130
Dialectic function, 78
Dialectic process, 82
Dilemma (The interviewers), 104
Dynamic information-gestalt, 113, 114, 138
Dynamics of the scene, 114, 120

Ego-alien, 104
Emergency interview, 110, 111
Emergency situation, 107
Empathy, 116, 117, 139
Enlightened patient, 49

Focal conflict, 133
Focal diagnosis, 119

Gestalt processes, 93–102
Good motivation, 42

Information-gestalt, 34, 113, 133
Information processes, 119
Insights based on experience, 27
Integrative activity, 51
Intellectual insights, 27

Language-gestalt, 140, 141
Learning interview, 122

Material-gestalt, 93, 95, 114

Narcissistic fantasies, 92
Negative results, 103
New information, 114

Objective information, 26, 33, 114
Objective perception level, 115
One-time counseling, 132
One-time therapeutic contact, 132
One-way mirror, 138
Origin of mental illness, 65

Passing identification, 113
Patient and his illness, 63
Personal intuition, 118
Postconstruction, 120
Prefield of the interview, 43
Prefield phenomena, 30
Preinterview, 55, 58
Presentation process, 94
Progressive development, 64
Psychotherapeutic work-field, 45

Readiness for treatment, 127
Regressive development, 64
Regression in the service of the ego, 117
Regressive participation, 82
Responsibility for aftereffects, 109

Scenic ego function, 82, 83, 126
Scenic elements, 108
Scenic or situational information, 27, 33, 123, 124
Scenic understanding, 82
Sense structures, 94
Sent-on-ahead patient, 43
Short-term therapy, 133, 134
Situational evidence, 81, 82
Situational perception, 115
Social sickness, 43
Stress of suffering, 39
Subjective information, 27, 33
Subjective perception, 115, 116
Suitable patient, 45

Teaching interview, 122
Technique of the prefield, 54
Temporary identification, 117
Therapeutic ego-splitting, 117
Therapeutic interview, 131–135
Threshold situation, 113, 114, 117, 118, 120, 122, 132, 133
Training problems, 137–141
Transference, 117

Unconscious communication, 42
Unconscious motivation, 41
Unproductive patient, 47, 78, 103
Unusual answers, 79